SURFIN(

To our friend Buje

SURFING
In Search of the Perfect Wave

Peter Diel & Eric Menges

Meyer & Meyer Sport

Original title:
Surfing – Auf der Suche nach der perfekten Welle
– Aachen: Meyer und Meyer Verlag, 1999
(Adventure Sports)

British Library Cataloguing in Publication Data
A catalogue record for this book is available from the British Library

Diel / Menges
Surfing – In Search of the Perfect Wave
Maidenhead: Meyer & Meyer Sport (UK) Ltd., 2008
ISBN: 978-1-84126-241-3

© 2000 by Meyer & Meyer Sport (UK) Ltd.
2nd, revised & updated edition 2008
Aachen, Adelaide, Auckland, Budapest, Cape Town, Graz, Indianapolis,
Maidenhead, New York, Olten (CH), Singapore, Toronto
Member of the World
Sport Publishers' Association (WSPA)
www.w-s-p-a.org
Printed and bound by: B.O.S.S Druck und Medien GmbH
ISBN: 978-1-84126-241-3
E-Mail: verlag@m-m-sports.com
www.m-m-sports.com

Contents

FOREWORD

On a trip to the South Pacific, we were surfing with a group of Australians on a remote reef in Fiji. During a wave lull, as we started chatting they asked where we came from. The answer, "... from Europe" caused a few puzzled looks, and we could see big question marks appearing over the heads of the Australians – "do you guys have any waves?"

Of course, these days there are thousands of surfers in Europe. France, Spain, Portugal, UK and even Germany all have professional surfers on the professional surfer circuit. This said, for most people living away from the coast in Europe (like us – the authors), surfing is rather an unusual sport, and there have been many occasions when it has been necessary to start explaining what surfing is all about. "No, not surfing the Internet, (whoever thought up this term should be punished anyway), no we do not use a sail. Yes, exactly that – riding the waves – just like in Hawaii."

On top of all that, here we are, two landlocked Euros, writing a book about surfing. However, we believe that the experience we have gathered during a long learning process will be useful to surfers and to beginners, who have not grown up by the sea or live there. Indeed, it does require particular effort and, above all, regular travel to become a surfer. But the message we give you is that anyone can learn surfing and have lots of fun doing it.

People are continually discovering this fascinating sport. Although snowboarding (surfing on snow) and skateboarding (surfing on the road) originally evolved as alternatives for surfing, there are today many skate- and snowboarders, who are still only just now discovering surfing as a sport. The characteristics of these sports are very similar and many of the movement sequences resemble each other.

Surfing is addictive

Watch Out!

(Photo: Hilton, Billabong)

There is the unforgettable and unbelievable kick when you snowboard through untouched powder, get big air in a half pipe, or successfully come out of a tube on a wave.

We have been surfing for about 25 years and have taught many how to surf. "Just do it!" – is definitely the right approach to surfing. Experience has shown, however, that a considerable amount of time, hassle and injury can be saved if some theoretical basework is done before heading out into the ocean. Well, you guessed it. Now is the moment to invest some time and read about the basics of wave riding. We are not going to try and teach you using scientifically proven methods.

On the contrary, we would like to offer some theory, however rather use a few real life experiences, anecdotes and stories from the surfing world to explain what it is all about. This book has been written with the beginner as well as the advanced in mind. The beginner will not have to continually bore the "cool surfers" with basic questions such as "Why do you tie that rope to your foot?" He will not make the whole beach erupt in laughter by waxing the wrong side of the surf-board (the underside). The advanced surfer will find some tips in our book that will help him progress on his way to becoming a genuine hardcore surfer.

A few years ago we decided to live our greatest dream - a journey round the world in search of the perfect wave. Our trip took us from Bali to Australia, New Zealand, Fiji, Tahiti, USA and to Mexico. Believe us - the perfect wave does exist. However one will never surf the same wave twice because every wave is different to the next. To make your search for the perfect wave a little easier, our book includes details of various surfing destinations in this world. We will provide you with many little yet often important tips to increase the fun factor on your travels and help you find your way in unfamiliar countries and waters.

A famous surfer once answered the question on who he thought was the best surfer in the world by replying, "The best surfer in the world is the one having the most fun." But, be careful, surfing is addictive! Once you have ridden your first glassy, long, green wave you will have nothing but surfing on your mind. So "Surf hard and respect the ocean." Enjoy reading this book!

N.B. To avoid repetition and easier reading; whenever the male pronoun is used the female form is equally meant to be included.

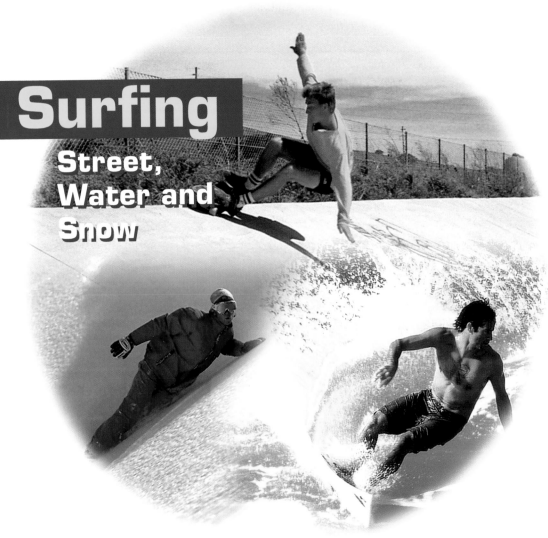

Surfing

Street,
Water and
Snow

**(Photos: Street – Menges & Diel,
Water – Joli, Snow – Xandi Kreuzeder, Chiemsee)**

THE ORIGIN OF SURFING

Even today the Hawaiians and the Tahitians still argue over the origin of surfing. One thing is sure – it started in Polynesia. Just exactly when surfing started there, however, is still a little uncertain and not proven. There are indications in native songs that this spectacular water sport was already being carried out in the 15th century. So, even before the white man placed foot on the Polynesian shores, waves were being ridden there. On his sea travels in 1777, Captain James Cook was the first white man to enjoy watching the Polynesian natives playing with the waves.

Thanks to one of their successors, the Hawaiian Duke Kahanamoku, surfing became so popular in our time. The "Duke" was an excellent swimmer and won several Olympic gold medals for the USA. On a visit to Australia, the "Duke" also demonstrated what he was capable of when it came to using a board. Riding waves – surfing – became increasingly popular from that moment on and spread across to California, New Zealand, South Africa and to Europe.

There are, of course, many more highly influential and legendary surfers who should be named here, like for example the American Greg Noll, "da Bull" – the big wave legend who rode one of the biggest waves of all times already in the 60s, or "the Gull ", Australian Mark Richards – who won four consecutive world titles in the seventies and eighties on his twin fin surfboards. Then there is Nat Young – the Australian surfing legend who introduced a new much more radical, manoeuvre oriented surfstyle, as well as of course the Michael Jordan or Tiger Woods of this sport , "his Eightness" the incredible, eight times (and counting) world Champion Kelly Slater – who is writing surfing history as you read this, and so on and so forth. But this is not a history lesson rather a surf lesson, so let's get on with it.

(Photo: Menges/Diel)

SURFING FOR BEGINNERS

Now you know where wave riding comes from. But how are you going to turn yourself into a second Duke? Well, nothing is guaranteed, but the following sections will help for sure.

How to Start

Alright, you have decided to become a surfer. Sounds good. Just think of all those unreal pictures on television and in the magazines! Looks really cool! But, unfortunately, it is not as easy as many top surfers make it look. The multitude of different factors that make it possible to actually stand up on a board and glide on a wave, without a sail and without footstraps, turn the first steps into an uphill struggle.

But don't give up just yet. Although many hours will be spent sitting in freezing water waiting for the waves that never came, and with your motivation close to zero, all of a sudden all will come together. The right wave, the correct paddling speed, no one in the way – and there you are – standing, surfing your first wave. What a feeling. So never give up. It is well worth the effort.

1.1 Requirements

Who can learn to surf? Basically anyone who can swim! For surfing, the size of the body is relatively insignificant. Actually, short surfers have a little advantage because of their somewhat lower centre of gravity. Although you will mainly find male surfers, the amount of women in surfing (in particular in the wake of the movie Blue Crush) is ever increasing as women can just as easily learn to surf. Irrespective of whether you are a man or a woman you must have a lot of patience and endurance. Surfing demands skill, timing and knowledge about waves, currents and the sea bottom. Surfing can sometimes be a little dangerous, but if you are well prepared and are aware of your own physical

That's You!

... in a few years

(Photo: Billabong, Jason Childs)

Anyone can surf

Ineika Surf School Fuerteventura (Photo: Menges & Diel)

and psychological limits, even as a beginner you will have a lot of fun.
Oh yes, and one more thing. You better start saving money for your first big surfing trip to Australia, Bali or Hawaii.

1.2 Equipment

1.2.1 The Right Surfboard for the Beginner

Selecting the right surfboard is a major factor for getting fun out of surfing, whether you are a beginner or an advanced surfer. The first surfboard should be long, thick and wide. The length and thickness gives the board more buoyancy, allowing you to paddle faster, and thereby helping you to catch a wave more easily. The width gives you extra stability when standing up. Either a longboard, or a hybrid or so-called Mini-Malibu is the most suitable board for the beginner. A typical longboard is between 9 and 10 foot long, 22 inches wide and between 3-4 inches thick. Let's stay with the English measuring system as this is most commonly used when boards or waves are described. But for those more used to metric measurements – 1 foot = 30.48 cm and 1 inch = 25.4 mm – thus we can easily translate the board into metric. A hybrid sits somewhere in between a longboard and a shortboard. It is about 6.5 to 8 feet long, 21-22 inches wide and 2.5-3.5 inches thick.

Besides the dimensions, there are a few other things to take note of. The board should not be too heavy and, above all, it should have no sharp edges e.g from previous repairs. Most injuries in surfing are caused by your own or by some other person's board. The most dangerous parts of the board are the tip of the nose and the fins. Thus the nose should be rounded and the fins should have no sharp edges (if necessary smoothe off the edges with sandpaper or get a board with those hard rubber fins). For a beginner it does not matter whether the board has one, two or three fins. The rails of the board should similarly also be smoothly rounded.

A surfboard is made out of a polyurethane foam core with a fibreglass laminate on the outer surface. The glass is easily damaged so therefore a surfboard must always be handled carefully. The ceiling of the surf shop is a classic for the first

Long, wide and thick

Typical beginners' boards

(Photo: Sigi Opitz, Ineika Funcenter)

ding when you lift a brand new board up for inspection. So watch out! If, despite all the good advice and the greatest care, you have damaged the board somehow, you must get it fixed as quickly as possible. Otherwise the foam core mentioned earlier will soak up water, and after a while, the board will become heavier, develop brown spots and simply will be no more fun to surf.

When buying a second-hand board you must check the board for any unrepaired cracks on the surface, that the fins and fin plugs are firmly fixed and that the foam is not lifting at any place. Brown coloured spots mean that water has already penetrated into the board. Also cracks that run right from one side to the other of the board can mean that the board has been broken in two before and will propably break again soon. So keep your fingers off.

A good alternative to purchase is to rent a board on the spot. Many surfing shops have, amongst other things, boards especially for beginners to hire. Also most snowboarding or windsurfing shops can possibly be of help in the search for a board to hire. But remember: long, thick, wide and no sharp edges!

1.2.2 The Wetsuit

The amount of time you will be able to spend in the water while having a go at surfing will largely depend on your clothing – the wetsuit. Especially when the conditions are good there is nothing worse then to start freezing after only five minutes in the water.

Wetsuits are made from a kind of rubber called neoprene. Unlike the so-called 'dry-suits' often used for windsurfing, which keep the body dry and protect the whole body from the cold water, neoprene suits work on a different principle. Water gets trapped between the rubber and the body and is then warmed by your own body temperature. However the next time you go under, the warm water is flushed out and changes place with fresh cold water, which is then warmed up again. The wetsuit must fit snugly on the body so that not too much water can penetrate i.e., the body does not have to warm up too much water. The suit should also sit relatively tightly on the arms, round the neck and the legs. The thickness of the neoprene determines how much the coldness of the water and the wind can reach the body from the outside.

New wetsuit materials allow maximum flexibility

European Junior Champ Marlon Lipke at full stretch

(Photo: Dago Lipke, The Surf Experience)

This brings us to another important feature of a wetsuit - comfort. Too close a fit makes movement in the water difficult, and you will want to move a great deal. The same applies to thick suits that are on the one hand very warm, but on the other also very heavy and unflexible. Many of the neoprene suits used by windsurfers or divers are therefore unsuitable for surfing. The thickness of the neoprene should be not more than 3 mm unless you are going to surf in extremely cold waters. The arms and legs of most surfing suits are 1 mm thinner than the rest. Very often you will find a number combination on the suit e.g., 3/2. This means 3 mm neoprene on the body part and 2 mm on the arms and legs.

Surfing suits come in various combinations, for example the 'full suit' or 'steamer' with long legs and sleeves, or the 'spring suit' with short sleeves and legs. To begin with use a suit with long legs. The sleeves can be either long or short. Long sleeves keep the warmth in but limit movement when paddling. If you choose a suit with long sleeves make sure it stretchs well around the shoulders and arms to allow for easier paddling.

The final decision is obviously dependent on the price but also your personal warmth requirements (skinnier people loose heat much quicker), where you are going to use it and of course what you look like in it (the Captain Kirk look remains a classic).

You will often find that you develop a rash on certain parts of your body from wearing the wetsuit. This is caused by the neoprene rubbing against your skin. To protect yourself you can get a special T-shirt made out of Lycra or a similar material – so-called wet-shirts or rash guards that are worn under the suit. Smearing Vaseline on the sensitive places offers another solution to prevent the rubbing. Whilst the latest wetsuits really do not require any of those anti-rash measures you can also wear the Lycra shirt without the suit to protect yourself against sunburn.

TIP

Just a few tips to help extend the life of your wetsuit! Whenever possible, after each use, you should rinse your suit in fresh water. You should also never leave your suit out to dry in the sun. It is perfectly sufficient to hang it on a clothes hanger or over a washing line in the shade. The water will automatically run out and it will dry without the aid of the sun.

If you do not want to buy a wetsuit straight away, try checking out the local surf shops where you can often find a decent suit for hire.

1.2.3 Wax and Leash

Wax

For a windsurfer it is the foot straps, for the snowboarder it is the binding and for the surfer it is the wax. Wax prevents the surfer from slipping off the wet board, which is obviously wet when in the water. Each time, before you go into the water, the whole upper-side of the board must be completely waxed. The rear two-thirds of the board are important (this is where the feet stand) as well as the side edges of the forward two-thirds (this is where you hold the board when you duck-dive through the waves). There is different wax for different water temperatures. You should use soft wax for cold water and harder wax for warm water. Most wax comes labelled as "cold water", "cool", "warm water" or "tropical". Make sure the surface of the board is not hot from the sun before you wax it. If this is the case simply hold the board in the water before you start waxing. You can do the same with a piece of wax that has been sitting in the sun and become soft.

If the board, at some stage, gathers a thick hardened surface after repeated waxing, it is sufficient to roughen up the surface with a so-called wax comb (you should buy one of these when you purchase your first piece of wax). By doing this the wax will become grippy again. If you run out of wax and you have left your wax comb in the car, you can also use some wet sand to roughen up some old wax.

Many surfers use a so-called 'grip deck' glued on to the board just about where the rear foot is placed. This is a development of the 'rubber daisies' that your mother used to put in the bottom of the bathtub so that 'little darling' would not slip. The grip deck gives your rear foot extra grip during powerful turns and saves you from having to wax your whole board everytime you hit the water. As a beginner however you might want to stick to waxing as you will hardly place your feet in the same spot everytime you stand up. It is therefore hard to predetermine just exactly where the grip deck should be stuck on the board. We will return to this in the section later on 'Equipment for the Advanced'.

Leash

The leash is an extremely practical and pleasant accessory. It resembles a lead made out of rubber. One end is attached to the end of the surfboard and the other end is fixed to the surfer's ankle using a Velcro fastener. The leash saves a lot of trouble and effort if you fall off the board or you have to let go of it. You will not have to swim all the way back to the beach to get your board after you have fallen off, simply because it is actually fixed to your ankle.

When buying the leash make sure it is equipped with a Velcro fastener with a simple opening mechanism. If the leash gets caught up in something in the water you must be able to open it with one quick movement (more about this in the section 'Equipment for the Advanced'). At the end where the leash is fixed to the board there should be a so-called 'railsaver'. This is made from a piece of strong tear proof textile, about 20 cm long, which prevents the leash from cutting into the polyester side of the rails when the board is pulled back . At the end of the railsaver, the leash is attached to the board through the so-called 'plug' using a nylon rope. If you have to knot this piece of nylon you should use your very best mega-double sailor's knot. What good is the best leash if the knot slips and you are left there with your leash strapped around your ankle without a board attached to it?

But watch out! As much as it is nice not to continually keep losing your board, to have a 2 m solid hard object (your surfboard) strapped to your leg in the water is pretty dangerous. The leash is very elastic. If the board is washed away by a solid wave the leash can be stretched to its utmost limit. When the wave passes, the board can shoot back like a harpoon. This usually happens exactly at the moment when you have just surfaced after a long hold down and come up for the long awaited deep breath, and you are thinking "Uhhh! Where's my board?" Many of us have collected a few real "smashing" looking scars this way. To avoid this, you should always surface with your hands on your head and your arms shielding your face. At the same time keep your eyes open and look around to see where your board is coming from in order to catch it. You should try to always automatically shield your head when surfacing, because not only the board of a beginner has the habit of shooting back.

1.3 Preparation

Surfing is a very strenuous and physical sport. Therefore some preparation at home is important. Surfing is much more fun if you are physically fit. You can paddle longer without tiring and therefore you can surf longer. You can lose your fear of being held under by a wave if you have practiced diving and holding your breath under water in the swimming pool beforehand. Some surfers say that the best training for surfing is simply surfing. Of course this is easy to say if you live five minutes away from the beach in Australia or California and can keep yourself fit by surfing on a daily basis. But for those of us who live away from the ocean and perhaps are only able spend a few weeks surfing; it is essential to carry out some preparation. Who wants to return to the beach after the first wave because your arms feel like jelly?

The main muscles that are used in surfing are the shoulder, back and upper arm muscles. The chest and neck muscles are also used a lot – in general the whole of the upper body is brought into play. The most tiring thing in surfing is not the actual surfing but the continuous paddling (for longer rides and lots of manoeuvres the leg muscles also play an important role). If you already own a board, you should practice paddling on your local lake. This way, you can get also get a feeling for the correct position on your board on home ground. A friend of ours ties up his surfboard with the leash to the side of the swimming pool and practices paddling on the spot – this is also a way. For those who have not yet got a surfboard (or pool), or find it embarrassing to turn up at the local lake with a surfboard, we recommend regular swimming as the best preparation for surfing. The most useful stroke is the crawl and in particular when you keep your head out of the water like the water polo guys do. This uses practically the same muscles as the paddling movement. Besides this, swimming longer distances underwater and training your lungs is very helpful as well. Other then swimming, press-ups and similar exercises will be useful, preferably done in front of the television with a surfmovie playing.

Something that can be done easily at home is determining your preferred way of standing on the surfboard. If you have been snow- or skateboarding before, you will know already whether you stand naturally with your left foot (regular foot) or with the right foot (goofy foot) forward. For those who do not yet know which foot to place foward there are two simple ways of finding out. The first is jumping up from a press-up into a sideways standing position as if you were leaping onto the surfboard. Most of the time, your subconscious will automatically find the correct position for you. The important thing is not to spend too long in the press-up position thinking about it – just simply jump up straight away.

The second way, concerns your so-called 'take-off leg'. This will always stand to the rear since, when surfing, this leg is the one that needs the most power. To find this out simply take a run and jump as if you were going for a basketball slam dunk, or doing a long jump over a puddle. The take-off leg is the one with which you lead off when jumping. If, after all this, you are still not quite sure, you should simply rely on the result of your first attempt. Some time or other you may notice that when you stand up on the surfboard you are continually getting entangled in the leash. This is because, despite everything that your subconscious (and our smart advice) told you, your left foot is the one that belongs to the rear. This is the moment that you turn out to be a goofy after all.

Ideal Training Ground

A permanent Wave

Quirin Rohleder river surfing in Munich (Photo: Uli Scherb, Wavetours)

2 The First Wave

Now you have the right surfboard, a cozy wetsuit, you have waxed your board, you have been swimming up and down, over and under water in the swimming pool, and now you are standing on the beach. You are ready to go but isn't there something still missing? Well of course! – It is the right wave.

2.1 The Right Wave for the Beginner

If you listen to other surfers, you will often hear, "There are some unreal waves out there – just perfect lines", and so on and so forth. You immediately want to grab your surfboard and paddle out. But there are waves and waves and not every wave is surfable. Even more important, what should the beginner be watching out for? Waves which look straight out of the latest surfing magazine often hide substantial danger. So do not just paddle out anywhere. Let's begin with the search for your first wave and make sure we know what to avoid.

To start with the waves should not be very big. This means that when you watch a surfer who is riding a wave, the wave should not be 'overhead' i.e., higher than the head of a surfer riding in an upright position. Although you should start your first few attempts mainly in white water or foam of larger broken waves, large waves further out usually also mean strong currents all along the beach. Strong currents can be dangerous and the beginner should try and avoid them. He will also often have difficulty in actually recognising strong currents.

It is therefore very important to spend some time just watching and observing the sea and its movements. If there are surfers in the water note whether they are being pulled out to sea rapidly when they paddle out. Surfers, who are further out, waiting for a wave may be paddling 'on the spot' in order to hold their position. This is an obvious indication that there is a strong current running through the line up.

Many beaches with lifeguards have a warning system. Sometimes flag signals are used to indicate sea dangers on any particular day. The beginner should try and seek some information on the day's conditions from the local lifeguards and above all should take their advice regarding currents and other dangers very seriously, simply because these girls and guys know best.

Many beaches also have boundary flags that indicate the swimming zone and non-surfing zone. You should definitely keep clear of these zones. If you disregard the zones you could find yourself having to hand your surfboard over to the life-guards faster then you can say "Baywatch".

Back to your first wave. If there are swimmers outside their marked off zones, make sure you stay clear of them, as they have no idea how fast and dangerous a loose surfboard (even on a leash) can be. Preferably try and get at least 50 meters between you and the next swimmer. Generally make sure that wherever you want to practice there are not many swimmers, boogie-boarders or surfers around in the water. The beginner needs lots of space. It goes without saying that you should not venture off into the wide wet far away from all the life-saving Baywatch models either. Someone must be available to keep a watching eye on you.

Now to the wave itself. As a beginner you should look for the foam of the wave. The foam that appears on the top of the wave, as it breaks should roll down conti-nuously as the wave travels towards the beach. As it reaches the beach it should run out smoothly. Waves that build up again and pound the shoreline as they break on to the beach (called 'shore breaks') are dangerous. Breaking your fin, board or body made easy!

Now a word about the sea bottom. The best waves for beginners break on to sandy beaches. This is not because of their quality. The reason is more that, in comparison to other bottom types, they will actually present less danger of hurting you. Waves that break on to reefs or along submerged reefs are totally unsuitable for the beginner. Areas with rocks or a harbour wall, a pier or similiar objects lining the shore are also unsuitable – unfortunately some of the best waves are found in these areas. But do not lose heart!

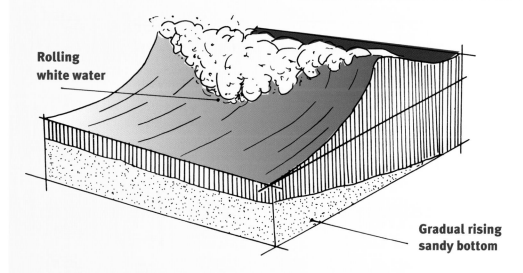

Rolling white water

Gradual rising sandy bottom

Gentle breaking wave on sandy bottom

(Drawing: Stefan "Muli" Müller)

2.2 Get Ready (on the Beach)

So you thought you could just simply jump in the water and paddle out? You are joking?! Well, first of all here are a few dry exercises for you to practice on the beach. This will make sure that you turn yourself into a complete beach-clown – but so what? Not only as a starter some warming-up exercises help avoid sprains and cramps. Start with the muscles that you use for paddling i.e., the arm and shoulder muscles.

You can also try out on the beach how to lie on the board while paddling. Put your surfboard down on the sand and push the fins into the sand so that you can lie down without breaking them. You should lie on the board with your chest somewhere just forward of the middle of the board. You should lie with head, shoulders and chest raised to form a hollow in the back. The actual paddling movement is very similar to the arm movement when doing the crawl in the pool. Keep your fingers together and pull the arms to the rear alongside the surfboard. Make sure that you pull all the way through – from the tip of the board right through to the full extension of your arm and out of the water (out of the sand in this case). Your legs should be kept together and your toes stretched out to the rear. The best thing to do is to keep your shin slightly raised out of the water so that the water resistance is brought to a minimum. This position is very strenuous for the beginner and the back muscles will quickly tire. Usually after a few days of intensive paddling, however, you will have built up most of the necessary muscles.

Now let us look at standing up. You should also practice this on the beach to start with. Lay down on the surfboard in the sand as already described above with your head up and your shoulders hollowed etc. Grab the rails with your hands at about the spot where your shoulders are in relation to the board. Your arms will be slightly angled in this position. Now we come to actually standing up. Press-up from the board and jump with both feet at once on to the surfboard. You must jump into a sideways stance with your feet well apart. The forward foot should be a little in front of the middle of the board and your rear foot about 30 cm from the tail of the surfboard. To practice this, do a press-up and then jump up into the standing position. Later the action must become one flowing movement i.e., as you press up with your arms, the jump into the standing position is done almost simultaneously.

It is important that this movement becomes automatic so that when you are in the water you do not have to think about it at all – nothing like 'Err, well – what was it? Hold on to the leash, press-up or what?" Keep on practicing jumping into the standing position until it becomes a natural thing to do. Far better to look a bit of a joker now, but to style down the waves later! All set? Now start walking in the direction of the water. I bet you thought you would never get there!

2.3 How Do I get out?

When we say "Get out" or "Out" in further sections of this book we mean "Get out on the sea!" The opposite is to "Go in!" which means getting back to the beach and into the arms of your girl- or boyfriend.

For your first day of surfing you have hopefully selected a sandy beach with little or no shore break and where the white water of the waves breaking further out, rolls more or less gently right up on to the beach. This is important because the white water creates a natural barrier for you. If your technique is not good enough to push through this white water, you will never reach the somewhat dangerous area where the large waves are breaking. It is another story with waves that break on a reef bottom. You can often paddle right around the white water and get out amongst large outside waves without even getting your hair wet. All of a sudden you are sitting in the line up between the other surfers and in the middle of some moving water mountains wondering what the hell you are supposed to do.

So the big question really is: "How do I get out as far as necessary? "

2.3.1 Entering the Water

After a warm-up, put your leash on – goofys on the left ankle and regulars on the right. Now pick up your surfboard. The best way is to carry it under your arm on the side where you wear your leash. The leash will dangle between the end of the board and your foot. It is too easy to get caught up in your leash and fall over, which really is not a very cool thing to do. To avoid this, grab the leash roughly about the middle of its length with the same hand that you are holding the board. Doing this effectively halves the length of the leash, and it does not tumble about any more. Now choose a spot where you can walk out as far as possible to meet the white water coming in. Keep your surfboard still under your arm as you enter the water. Do not drag it along in the water. You should keep control of your surfboard at all times, otherwise even a small wave will smash it against your shin or some other part of your body. Now we are slowly getting closer – do not panic when the first white water comes rushing in. Avoid holding the board in front of you as a shield. Otherwise the next wave will simply smash it into your face. The board must remain horizontal, held next to your body with the fins pointing downwards. Once you are far enough out in the water and you have walked through the first few waves, you can lie down on the surfboard and begin to paddle.

2.3.2 Paddling

Sorry to tell you, but paddling is really what you will actually be doing for most of the time when you go surfing. You will be paddling out to sea, paddling to get over a wave, paddling to catch a wave and paddling back to the beach etc. Sooner or later it is going to be as natural as walking.

When you start your first paddle attempt, make sure that the surfboard lies flat on the water. The nose of the board should stick out of the water a little. Not too much otherwise you will be pushing water in front of you rather than gliding over it. You would not be able to reach the right speed when paddling for a wave. Do not forget what we practiced on the beach: chest just above the middle of the board, head up, back and toes stretched out, shins just out of the water and pull through well with the arms. It all sounds simple, and it is, but you should never underestimate paddling. Paddling is one of the most important things in surfing. Some will of course say, "But what about standing up and riding the wave?"

Well, of course this is all important, but if you do not build up enough speed when paddling because you are not lying on the board properly, or you are using the

Wrong paddling position

Too far back on the board, feet and legs apart

Right paddling position

Chest in the middle, back stretched out, feet together and out of the water

(Photos: Menges & Diel)

wrong paddling technique, you will not even catch a wave. You will be surprised when for the first time you paddle next to a really good surfer and suddenly find that in fact he is paddling and moving around in the line-up so much quicker and more efficiently than you are. Perfecting the paddling movement and building up the necessary muscles are therefore very important for the beginner. If you want to be a good surfer, you must be in a position to be able to paddle fast and effectively. When you have finally made it out the back, sitting on your board waiting for a wave and finally the right one is coming, you must be able to quickly lay down on your board and match the speed of the wave with a few paddling strokes. If not, the wave will simply pass by underneath you. But more on catching a wave a little later.

After you have slipped off your board a couple of times and still paddling on the same spot, all of a sudden, slowly for sure, you will start moving forward and paddle your board out to where the waves are.

2.3.3 Dealing with Broken Waves

As a beginner, of course, you do not want to go right out the back where the big waves are breaking. You should rather try surfing the white water of broken waves further inside during your first attempts. But despite this, sometime or other, you will have to venture further out and over the first wave. When looking at bigger waves you will often ask yourself how on earth you are going to go through, over or under them without receiving the beating you have not even yet deserved. However, using the right technique – 'duck-diving' – which we will describe later – and the correct amount of endurance and practice, it will not be such a big deal for you anymore. Duck-diving is quite a complicated technique and it can take a while before you really master it. This is why you should, initially, use the beginner techniques to get over the first few lines of white water. According to how far you have managed to walk out through the shallow water and how deep the water is where you are, there are several methods. If you are still able to stand in the water and a wave is rolling towards you, simply push yourself off the ground and lay the board in front of you and on to the foam, pushing and supporting yourself on the board as far as possible. Make sure you get a good grip on your board beforehand. If you are further out to sea, and you are already lying on the board and paddling, there are also several ways of pushing through waves. Firstly you can get off the board and simply dive through the wave without the board. Pull the board along behind you not holding on to the leash but, to avoid having your fingers squashed, by grabbing the railsaver (you know that piece of nylon which connects the leash to the board). Another way is to do a kind of press-up on the board. This is done by paddling with speed towards the white water. Just before you meet the wave, you press up your body from the board – like in a press-up – so that the water can pass between your body and the board. This method, however, will only work in small waves.

If you are facing a larger wave, in the split second as it breaks just in front of you or over you, you have probably already forgotten everything that we have explained anyway. You wish you were far away now! In such a case we recom-

Beautiful "Duck-dive"

(Photo: Bill Morris, O'Neill)

mend the emergency exit, or as it is called 'bail out'. Let go of your board and dive down as deep as you can. Not the ideal solution, but it is often the only way to make a quick getaway. It is essential that you make absolutely sure that no other surfer is behind you when you let go of the board and dive. The wave would slam your board straight into anyone paddling behind you.

This option is, therefore, really for an emergency only. Among surfers, letting go of the board is a foul. Other surfers can easily get injured this way. Do this in a crowded line-up and you are sure to raise the (sometimes violent) anger of not only the locals. Another downside is that it takes you much longer to gain control of the board after the wave has passed because, first of all, you have to pull the board back towards you, by which time normally the next wave set will have arrived.

By the way, please remember always to surface with your hands and arms protecting your head. Sometimes the board is immediately above you when you surface. If you do not have the protection of your arms and hands as you come up, eventually your board and your head are sure to get dented.

Another tip – when surfacing after bailing out you will want to pull your board back quickly but it often sticks in the water like a buoy or anchor not wanting to move at all. Don't panic – just swim a stroke or two towards the board. This releases the pressure on the board and the pull on the leash caused by the water pushing over it and allows you to quickly regain control.

2.4 How to 'Catch' a Wave?

You are now where you wanted to be from the start – on the ocean to surf. This means that, up until now, everything was just preparation, but now we can really get down to business. Let's catch a wave and go surfing! Lying, kneeling or stand...... oh well, OK, more of this later. But it does not matter which way you ride a wave. To surf, first of all you have to catch the wave and the wave has to take you with it. It all looks so simple, but it is not that easy. It is all a question of good timing and the right judgement of the approaching wave or white water.

First of all – a quick look at the sequence of actions:

You are sitting or lying on the board looking out to sea. A wave that looks surfable approaches. Paddling, you turn the board to point towards the beach. You glance over your shoulder to get a better look at the advancing wave, and at the same time you start paddling strongly towards the beach. The wave picks you up from behind and now you mobilise all your strength to increase your paddling speed. The wave pushes you and all of a sudden you are gliding towards the beach without you having to do anything. You are surfing.

Now that was simple, wasn't it? Nevertheless the part which gives most beginners great problems is paddling to catch the wave. Even more so later on when they have to stand up just at the moment they are being picked up by the wave.

2.4.1 Paddling for a Wave

Just imagine that you want to jump on to a (slow) moving train. You would be standing by the rails and, at the right moment – here we go – just jump on the train. It is more likely that you would run alongside the train, for a short time to reach the same speed as the train, and then, at the right moment, jump on. The more you can match the speed of the train, the easier it will be for you to jump on and hold on firmly.

Well, of course this comparison is a little far-fetched but it does serve to emphasise the key point about paddling for a wave.

The aim is to match, for a short moment, the speed of the wave by paddling.

It is only then that the wave will pick you up and take you along and will not simply pass by under you.

What exactly is the key? It is easy, speed is the key.

First of all let's return to the beginning of the situation we described where you were lying or sitting on your surfboard, gazing out to sea. As mentioned before the beginner should start off using the foam of a wave that has already broken. But do not be mistaken, this foam often has enough power to either throw you off the board or shoot you off towards the beach at breathtaking speed. Here we go. White water is approaching. You decide you are going to have a go at this one. You turn your board with a few paddling movements so that it is pointing straight towards the beach, and you begin to paddle forward. The main point here is to start doing this early enough. Of course if you watch the pro surfers it will appear that they do all of this at once and in the very last second. That is, when the wave is directly behind them they make a couple (maximum) of paddling strokes, and hey presto, there they are standing and surfing. You are not quite there yet. As a beginner you must start to paddle as early as you can see the wave moving towards you. This gives you more time to build up your speed. You paddle at full speed, glancing over your shoulder occasionally in order to judge how far away the wave still is. Now comes the critical moment. The wave is directly behind you and lifts the tail of the board up. Now you have to put every bit of strength you have left into it to increase your speed even further, and we mean every bit. Paddle as fast as you can. It is as if all those hours spent in the swimming pool were the training for this one moment.

Now this is when all beginners make the classic mistake of stopping paddling too early, namely as soon as they feel the board being lifted up behind them. The lifting of the board must not be the signal to stop, rather the starting gun to put down the pedal to the metal and paddle like mad. This is important. Even if you think you can feel that the wave is taking you, because everything starts to move a little faster around you, you still have to give two or three additional powerful strokes with your arms. And now – yes, now – the wave is taking you with it, and the fun begins.

Let's look at it once again:
- ◯ Start paddling towards the beach early and build up your speed.
- ◯ At the moment the wave picks you up from behind, mobilise all your strength and paddle like you were being followed by a shark.
- ◯ When you think you have caught the wave, make two to three additional powerful strokes.

Especially for the last point it is important that you have the right position on the board. If you are lying too far forward, just when the board is picked up from behind, the tip of the board will dig into the water (nosedive) usually resulting in a small somersault.

If you are lying too far towards the rear, it feels as if you had thrown an anchor overboard. The wave will then be too fast for you. It will run underneath or over the top of you. Generally speaking, you should tend to lie just a little to the front. It can well happen that you will do a nosedive, but the wave will tend to take you with it more easily than if you had been lying too far to the rear. You will eventually figure out how not to nosedive by shifting you weight backwards again a little straight after the take-off. All this of course after at least a dozen or so nosedives.

The start point for a successful ride is the right balance on the board. Take a little time practicing in calm water, exploring the ins and outs of the correct position. Earlier on we said that the beginner should start using the white water of a broken wave. However if you feel confident enough there is no reason why you should not try an unbroken wave. Our experience is that this will usually end up in a few funny wipe-outs, but that the beginner will develop a feeling for the waves quicker, and it is quite simply a lot more fun. So if you feel safe, and have been finding the white water rides a little boring, give it a try and paddle out to a real wave. However there are one or two things that you should watch out for, and which are different than when you were starting with the foam.

The size of the waves should be such that you do not get a funny feeling just looking at them. Also, even for the most daring, the size of the wave should not be more than a metre.

Take care – when you are standing on the beach everything looks different than when you are lying on your belly paddling towards a wave. All of a sudden, the waves look enormous. Lie down in front of a small child and look up (OK – just imagining this should do the trick). Even a one metre dwarf will look like a giant. It is the same with waves – so do not underestimate the surf.

Just like when you were paddling for the white water, you are now lying on your board and an unbroken wave is coming towards you. It still has its full height, and is not yet pushing any white water in front of it.

1

Paddle

3

Stand up

2 — Press up

4 — Surf!

(Photos: Sigi Opitz, Ineika Funcenter)

Now comes the tricky part. When you start paddling towards the beach, the wave has got to be just before it breaks. It should be very steep but not yet broken. This means that you have to judge, absolutely correctly, the speed of the incoming wave, and, at first, this is not at all easy to do. With a bit of luck, and having again done a few starts in the white water (because the wave broke too early), you will soon have this wired. If the wave breaks before it reaches you, use the foam to surf on, and paddle out a little further the next time – "Hey, I said just a little", said the surfing instructor just before his pupil disappeared over the horizon. If the wave runs through and under you and breaks a few metres past you, then wait for the wave a few metres nearer to the beach next time around. After a few attempts you will soon find just the right spot.

Naturally you can be guided by the other surfers around you. However, we have already mentioned that the beginner should keep away from other surfers; somewhere under supervision, but generally speaking with plenty of space around him for the first attempts.

This is important! If you find that a surfer is already riding on the wave that is approaching, do not start paddling at all. Wait for the next wave. A surfer who is standing has absolute right of way. Try to get out of the surfer's way. If you do not know which way is "out of the way", simply stay where you are and do not move about. Better surfers will then be able to avoid you. We will return later to discuss the exact right of way rules.

Back to paddling! Let us assume that you are at the right place, at the right time, and you have begun to paddle towards the beach also at just the right moment. The wave is about to break and it is directly behind you. The feeling of being picked up from behind by the wave is naturally much more intense than when starting with white water. After all, a metre high wave will lift you up a metre. Otherwise, the sequence remains the same. The wave lifts you up, and you put everything into paddling. This is your first wave – go for it! The wave pushes you forward and the speed picks up. Now for the famous last two powerful paddling strokes, and – whoops, the nose of the board digs into the water and you do the usual forward loop.

Never mind – just try again. Clearly, because the wave face is relatively steep, there is somewhat of an edge at the bottom.

As soon as you have made your two last paddling strokes, take a firm hold of the sides of the board and move your weight a little towards the rear. Again, here you will have to try several times to get the right feeling.

The most important thing, however, is that you actually catch a wave. Calling on our example at the beginning once again:
   – You have jumped on to the moving train, but now you have to manage to hold on to enjoy the ride.

2.4.2 Catching a Wave

I n this part of the book we are going to try to teach you something, that, to be honest, can only really be learned by trying it yourself. You may read this book over and over again but surfing can only be learnt by surfing, and not by doing some or other form of drill, or by reading clever books like this one. It is simply a question of going through the written descriptions and picking up a tip or two from us, so that the learning process is a little easier and quicker. If only you fall off your board a little less often because of our book, we will be smiling from ear to ear.

Surfing, in its broadest sense of gliding on a wave, can be done in several different ways. Simply lying down, kneeling, of course standing up, and even completely without a board – body surfing. The important ways for the beginner are lying down and generally of course the 'proper' way of surfing – standing up. The latter calls for a degree of balance, timing and above all practice. We will not go into surfing in the kneeling position, although there are a number of surfers, – so-called knee boarders – who have made this a speciality and who can do some very radical things in radical waves. Other than that, you should surf on your knees if you have not been able to make it to the standing position. This is then more or less rather by chance or in order to avoid a wipe-out. In short, we want you to become a 'real surfer', who, standing up on his board, can master the waves of this world. Now a few words about your first attempts at surfing lying down – just like the old saying "you've got to learn to walk before you can run".

2.4.2.1 The Prone Position

As a result of your paddling efforts, a wave has actually picked you up – but, what now? Quite simple – just enjoy the ride! Hold on to the sides of the board, and simply let it run, or as they say, 'Go with the flow'. You will notice at some point that you appear to be too heavy for the wave. The farther the wave travels away from the point where it broke, the less power it has. You are left behind, so to speak, and the wave runs through underneath you. If you are getting too close to the beach, just roll off the board so that, logically, you stop immediately. After your next successful attempt at catching a wave, try out a few things like the following. You can steer very simply by changing your centre of mass on the board. Because you will have both hands holding the sides of the board, you only need to lift it with your right (or left) hand and you will turn to the left (or right). Try surfing in a line across the foam. Now steer left or right so that you surf almost parallel to and along the line of the foam. This all serves to give you a feeling for the waves. How fast is the wave, and how should I change my balance so that I can glide along as far as possible? When all this gets a little boring, then it is time to ascend into the league of 'stand up surfers'.

2.4.2.2 Standing up

Surfing in the stand up position is actually what this book is all about. Even when the moment that you are standing and gliding on a wave lasts only a few seconds, the joy you experience will capture you. You will want more – and you will get more. The more you practice, the longer you will be able to ride on the wave – and these waves will, step-by-step, get even larger. But, first of all – back to the beginning.

Now that you know how to paddle for a wave, and how to surf lying down, the next step is just a little one. But, as Armstrong said when he visited the moon "One small step for man, but a large step on the way to becoming a surfer" or something like that.

OK! Let's get going: paddle, push down the accelerator and two final strokes ...?

STOP

Do you still remember all the dry land exercises, embarrassing as they were? The jumps-up into the stand from the press-up position? Never mind whether you are a goofy or a regular – i.e., with the right foot or the left forward. That is exactly what you have to do now. It really will now be an advantage if you did the exercises on the beach earlier once or twice too often. The key is automation. Back to the wave! Above all, it is important that you only try to stand up when the wave has really and truly picked you up. Generally, most beginners tend to try to stand up straight away, at the moment when the wave lifts them up and pushes them from behind. Because of this, we mention it over and over again, that when you think the wave has picked you up, you must make at least two further strong strokes. Otherwise, the wave will run away underneath you just as you try to stand up. This often has

(Photo: Uli and Martin, Wave Tours)

The critical moment
for Uli from Wave Tours

certain similarity with the sinking of the Titanic. On the relatively small surfboards, you cannot simply stand without the necessary forward momentum. Without the speed of the wave you will simply sink. So, only stand up when you really have the wave. Of course, you will fall off the first few times, despite having done all the dry land exercises often enough. This is all part of it. If you have equipped yourself from the beginning with a long, wide surfboard, then this will make everything much easier. It is easier to maintain your balance, and you will succeed quicker.

Then on your next surf trip, the board can already get a few centimetres shorter but for now, the large board is just right. There is always the possibility that you can adopt a kneeling position before you stand up. You will probably do this for the first few attempts anyway. However, this way of learning is not recommended. You quickly get used to kneeling before standing. This leads not only to cuts and to bruises of the knee and a damaged wetsuit, but also later on in fast and hollow waves, just at the moment when you need to stand up, you will waste a lot of precious time. This is why it is best to go directly from lying down to standing up. Your stance should be as wide as sensibly possible; this means that your front foot and your back foot should be placed relatively far apart from each other – but please, do not do the splits! If you have been snowboarding or skateboarding you will already know the best way to stand safely on the board. One surfer will have a somewhat broader stance, the other a slightly narrower one. Your back foot should be about 30 cm from the tail of the board, with your front foot placed just a bit in front of the middle. In the end, of course everyone stands slightly differently. The grip deck on the tail of the board gives a good indication where your rear foot should be. You just have to try it out. You will soon find your individual preference. If you stand too far back, you will brake the board too hard. The wave will run through underneath you because you will have lost momentum. If you stand too far forward the nose will dig into the water and whoops ... well, you already know this one.

For the first attempts, you should also bend and flex your knees as deeply as possible. This means you should not stand upright straight away. The centre of mass of your body will be lower and you can maintain your balance better.

And now the most important advice: practice, practice, practice, again and again and again. Above all never give up!
There will come a moment when you are suddenly standing and surfing and you

have no idea how you did it. We still remember the first real wave of a friend of ours, whose nickname funnily enough was "Fish". All week Fish kept falling off his board, had swallowed tons of water, and constantly swore about this "absolutely stupid" sport. We had both just ridden a wave and were paddling back out as Fish, standing up, came surfing towards us on a screamer of a wave. We will never forget the look on his face. He will probably not forget our completely puzzled looks either.

(Photo: Ashton Robinson)

Smile please, Peter!

Small Waves are fun too!

2.5 How Do I Get Back to the Beach?

We will assume that you have followed our advice and have chosen a sandy beach for your first attempts. This means that where you have entered the water you can easily come out again on to dry land. This is not always the case when you surf reef breaks and point breaks. You have just decided to stop your surfing session – for whatever reason – you are hungry, tired or cold. It is important that you never exhaust yourself completely. You must always have some reserves left as sometimes you may find a few obstacles on your way to the beach. So let's start with a safety tip:

If you ever find yourself in real difficulty, signal the SOS by waving at people on the beach or at other surfers, where possible, with both hands above your head.

Let's hope that you will never have to do this. The simplest way to get back to the beach is to ride a wave in the prone position, or to let yourself be pushed back to the beach by the white water of a broken wave. Here again do not forget to paddle to catch it. Try, as far as possible, to keep in the foam moving towards the beach. If you begin to lose momentum, you can always do a few additional paddling strokes. This will keep you on the wave even when it is really too weak to take you with it.

On the way home, you could meet the following problems:
1. Strong currents close to the beach.
2. The shore break.

The first one is not a real problem. If the white water is unable to carry you with it, you can paddle with your own strength to the beach. If there is a current running parallel to the beach (which is often the case when the white water falls away before you reach the shore), caused by the sandbanks where the waves break, getting back will be a little more difficult. The water breaks on to the sandbanks and runs away in a kind of basin. This can be quite deep at high tide. No waves break in this area, so you cannot use them to ride back to the beach. The water flows out of these basins sideways and creates currents. A tip! Never paddle against the current for a long time. Close to the beach you will be carried along several metres. Do not panic – simply go with the current yet constantly paddle in the direction of the beach. Sooner or later the current will let you go and you will succeed. But wait a minute, there is still a little obstacle – the shore break.

The shore break is the last obstacle. It can hide a certain danger. You cannot surf this wave because it breaks directly on to the beach. If you are still lying or standing on your board when it breaks, it means certain damage to your beloved surfboard. So be careful – many a board has been broken into two or more pieces by the shore break. The trick here is to paddle up as far as you can to the edge of the last break, then get off the board and support yourself on it. Lay one arm over the board to stabilise it, and swim using leg strokes only (like the breaststroke kick) to the beach. Wait for a smaller wave and let yourself be pushed on to the beach swimming along with the wave. The advantage is that you will end up standing in shallow water, and you already have your board under your arm and thus you can run out of the shore break impact zone before the next wave hits. Dependant on how strong the shore break is it may actually be advisable to even race out of the water. The treacherous thing about the shore break is that the broken waves run back into the sea and create a kind of reverse current, which tends to pull you back into the impact zone of the shore break. If you are stuck here, you will get a regular pounding. So, get off the board in advance and swim, and finally run away from the wave – so to speak.

If you have managed this last hurdle, you can take a deep breath. Now, your first surfing session was not all that bad, was it? If you listen very carefully you will surely hear the group Pearl Jam somewhere in the background singing, "Oh, I'm still alive".

Let's go surfing!

(Photo: Tim McKenna, Billabong)

3 Now Let's Surf!

Your first attempts at surfing will have been restricted to paddling for a wave and just riding down it. Arriving at the bottom of the wave face you will probably only surf for a few metres and then slow down and fall off. The reason for this is that your momentum after the take-off will be very high. You will move faster than the wave and will so to speak overtake it. When your momentum and speed drop the wave will catch up with you as it breaks, and usually you will be knocked off the board. For the first few take-offs and attempts at standing this is OK of course, but soon you should try to avoid only going straight. Try to surf to the left or right across the wave face shortly after you have caught it. This means you will no longer be surfing towards the beach but now parallel to it down the line of the breaking wave. You stay in front of the white water in the unbroken part of the wave.

The advanced surfer will build up speed by alternately swinging up and down the wave face. This looks really like riding the wave – he is a wave rider.

3.1 Riding a Wave

To be able to ride down the line of the wave it is important that the wave does not break along its whole length all at the same moment. The wave should break to the left or right. Along the length of the wave there should always be a part that has not yet broken. The surfer will always try to surf a wave in his mind and think of trying to keep in front of the wave's white water and foam. Sometimes the waves break too early and quickly so that the surfer has not have enough time to get in front of the breaking wave. The wave is "closing out" and the surf spot is not working and it may be worth checking another spot. If the wave slowly peels in one direction or the other, you should give it a go.

Viewing from the water in the direction of the beach when the wave breaks to the left we speak of a "left-hander" or a "left". If it breaks to the right then it is called a "right-hander" or a "right". This sounds logical enough, but it is often misunderstood. Remember – the direction of the breaking wave is described always from a viewpoint in the water looking towards the beach.

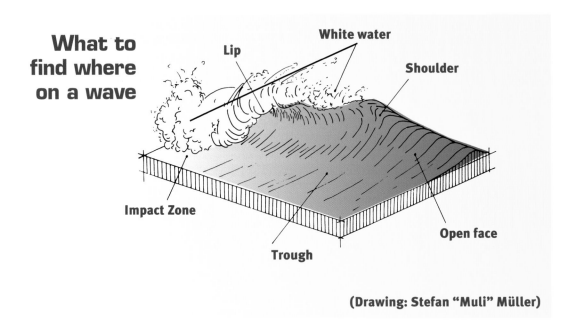

What to find where on a wave

White water

Lip

Shoulder

Impact Zone

Open face

Trough

(Drawing: Stefan "Muli" Müller)

A goofy-foot – someone who stands with the left foot to the rear – surfs a left facing the wave. He is therefore surfing "frontside" on his "forehand" as we say. The regular foot, conversely, will have his face to the wave if it is a right. If you surf with your back to the wave you are surfing "backside" on your "backhand". The difference is that most surfers find it easier to surf frontside along a wave. The sequence of movements is more natural on your forehand. The wave is always in sight, allowing you to react quicker when the wave changes. Many of the left breaking waves in the world were surfed for some time by goofys before a regular on his backhand mastered them one day. Meanwhile surfers and their equipment have reached such a high level, that surfing frontside or backside does only make a difference in particularly extreme wave conditions. Your first surfing experience, however, to keep it simple, should be done frontside on your forehand.

But how do you manage to surf along the wave rather then just down it?

There are two basic techniques. One is to paddle for a wave in an angle to the straight-ahead direction. The other way is to ride down the wave and then turn at the bottom of the wave up into the unbroken part of the wave. This latter technique is one of the most important manoeuvres for the advanced surfer – this is called the 'bottom turn'. A good bottom turn, is the efficient transformation of the speed gained from dropping down the wave into a good speed to surf along the wave face. A good bottom turn is often the key to a great ride. But more about this later. To begin with, you should try to paddle for a wave in an angle. This means that instead of paddling straight towards the beach, you paddle diagonally down the line of the breaking wave – dependent on the wave, left or right. Using a clock as a guide, with the beach at 12 o'clock, paddle left towards 10 o'clock, or to the right to 2 o'clock. If you have paddled fast enough and have not forgotten the all-important last two strokes, you will be moving almost parallel to the beach. You should try this in the prone position for the first few times, to get the feeling of actually moving sideways along the wave without losing speed.

Paddling for a wave in an angle is usually not the problem here. For the beginner it is more likely to be very difficult to recognise in which direction and where the wave is breaking. There is only one way out. Practice and keep watching the waves and other surfers. Try guessing which direction a surfer will take as you watch him paddle for a wave. So-called 'line-ups' are not only used by competent surfers to orientate themselves in the water, but can also help the beginners. In general, the area where surfers sit in the water waiting for a wave is also called the 'line-up'. Interestingly this is actually the first orientation point used to predict where the waves will break. Quite logical isn't it? Why else would the surfers be sitting just there?

However, "Line-up" can also mean a landmark on the beach, which can be used as a reference point on land when you sit in the water waiting for waves. A coloured beach umbrella, a particular shaped tree or some scrub on a hill or dune can all be used to line yourself up with once you are in the water. You will be able to judge whether you are drifting left or right just by constantly checking you position relative to your "line-up". If you find some good orientation points while you are still on the beach, later on when you sit out the back in the water you will find it easier to say which way the wave will break – to the right or to the left of your line-up. To summarise – orientation points on the beach can help you understand where you are going, where the waves are going and what is going on around you.

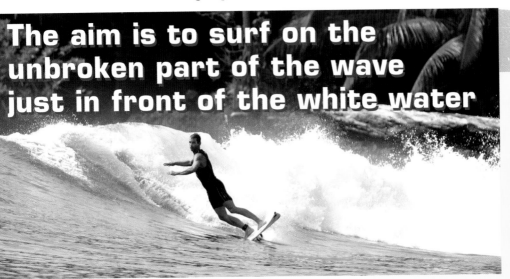

The aim is to surf on the unbroken part of the wave just in front of the white water

(Photo: Ashton Robinson)

3.2 The First Manoeuvres

To surf successfully along a wave, from beginning to end, it is important to learn the manoeuvres that will help you hold your speed so that you are always surfing in front of the white water. Let's carry on where we left off: You paddle for a wave in an angled direction, successfully stood up and are now up and riding in front of the white water. The wave is changing shape all the time. Sometimes the wall in front of you gets steeper and you speed up. It then becomes flatter again and you slow down. The degree of the slope of the wave face depends on the depth of the water. Shallow water creates steep waves. Sounds simple. But, what happens when after a slow section the wave runs into a quicker section? If you have not built up enough speed, the faster section will break before you reach it, or it will break over or on top of you, and your ride will be over.

There are different techniques of building up or dropping off speed. The latter is of particular interest when a slower section follows a fast one, and you are zipping away in front of it because of the speed you have built up already. But, first of all the most important point – building up speed. In advanced surfing, trimming your board is called 'pushing' or 'pumping' the board. You gain speed by alternately riding up and down the wave face. The initial speed of course comes from the take-off.

Basically, by placing your weight onto the back foot you will slow down, and onto the front foot, you will speed up. Let's assume that you are a regular foot, riding a wave to the right i.e., facing the wave (frontside). For a goofy-foot, the following will of course be the opposite. You are surfing diagonally along a wave (regular foot frontside). Normally your position on the wave face is approximately halfway between the trough of the wave and its upper lip or curl. You now lean a little towards the direction you want to go. The more you switch your balance, the more extreme your turn or curve will be. But easy ... gently does it! You lean slightly towards the base of the wave face i.e., to the left. You give a little pressure down-ward on to the forward foot, and thus begin surfing down the wave. At the bottom of the wave you have gained enough speed, and with a change of balance now towards the wave face i.e., to the right, you swing up the wave face again. You surf upwards until you begin to lose speed and start to slow down. Now you surf down the wave again and so on.

If you have caught a good long wave you can repeat this several times, achie-ving a sort of rhythm. This is good, because all the uphill and downhill move-ments (this is starting to sound like a book on snowboarding) should be done with no sharp turns, rather more a combination of fluid movements. Once you have successfully managed your first few longer rides you can try to unweight alternately in order to gain yet more speed. On top of the wave flex your knees. Just at the moment you begin to surf down, gently press down with the legs. At the foot of the wave face, the centrifugal force will have almost automatically made you flex your knees again. If you now change your centre of mass towards the top of the wave, and unweight the board at the same time, you will gain momentum as you move up the wave face. Back at the top, the wave will press your knees down together like a shock absorber. Now press down with the legs again and surf down the wave face. You will soon get the feeling for how the weighting and unweighting process works, because it is determined by the wave itself. The whole process is almost like when you get a child's swing in motion on your own. You can also imagine that you are on a snowboard or skis applying the classic up and down movement to go through turns. Above all, it is important that during each movement you keep your eyes on the point where your turn will lead or where you want to end up after your turn.

To end your ride, or if the wave closes out in front of you and you have to abort your ride, there are two ways of doing this. One is called the 'kick-out' or 'flick off', and is done by turning the board up the wave, over the top and over the back of it. Watch out here – doing this can catapult you into the air. Spectacular to watch for the spectator but dangerous for the surfer not only because the board is connected to the leash and the foot. You may land on your own board (thereby breaking it) or on another surfer. To avoid flying into the air, simply push down with the front foot as you reach the top of the wave, allowing you to actually ride over the back of the wave. Really cool, especially when you are able to lie down on your board just after you pushed over the wave and immediately begin to paddle out again after a good ride. The other way to exit a wave is to turn and ride towards the beach and leave the closed out section behind you. When the white water catches you either lie down on your board, hold on tightly and surf towards the beach on your belly, or jump off the back of the board, pushing it towards the beach as you do. Generally, the white water will wash over you and you will not get washed too far into the shore. You can now paddle quickly out to the line-up again.

The Bottom Turn

The 'bottom turn' is really only a turn at the bottom of the wave face. It is as important for the surfer as is the serve for a tennis player – for some a highlight of their talent, or for others 'just' the beginning for everything that follows. During the movements we have just described for the up and down on the wave face, you were already doing small bottom turns. A real bottom turn, however, means that at the foot of the wave you not only lean towards the wave a little, but you also apply so much pressure on the inside rail that the board actually goes through the turn on its edge or rail. The result is that you do not lose any momentum and you can continue surfing with full speed. This movement is very similar to carving when snowboarding. If you are leaning over far enough during the turn, your hand will often touch the water (– the rear hand in case of a forehand bottom turn). When you surf down a wave and, at the bottom, lead with your rear hand, pointing it in the direction of the water, you will automatically lay into the bottom turn just a little more. During the turn pressure and weight is always on the rail closest to the wave face – the inside-rail of the board. When you unweight and take the pressure off the rail, the turn is completed and you surf up the wave face again setting up the next move.

Weight on the inside rail

Backside Bottom Turn

(Photo: "Dr. Surf" Thomas Herold)

The Top Turn

By doing a good bottom turn you will have speed left to be able to surf up the wave face again. More than likely you will even have too much speed, so that you would shoot over the top of the wave if it were not for a manoeuvre that allows you to slow down a little and change direction right at the top of the wave and start descending again.

This is done by applying strong pressure on the rear foot. You give your rear leg an additional push to press the tail of the board through the turn as if you were trying to push the water away with the tail of your board. You simply push the tail through the turn. Your front foot is practically the pivot and the rear one steers through the move.

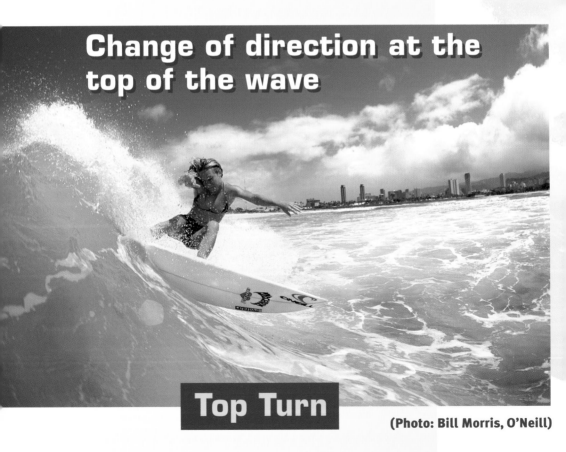

Change of direction at the top of the wave

Top Turn

(Photo: Bill Morris, O'Neill)

The Cutback

A further manoeuvre to reduce speed and not race away from the wave, is the 'cutback'. In its simplest form it is merely a turn in the opposite direction to the breaking direction of the wave. You will need the cutback if you are too far out on the shoulder of the wave i.e., you are too far away from the breaking curl of the wave. This can often be the case when a mellower, slower part follows a steep, fast part of the wave. The sequence in detail:

You are surfing along a wave, and notice that you have too much speed as you are riding too far out on the shoulder. You are not able to use this speed because in front of you the wave is starting to get relatively flat. Time for a cutback! You make a turn in the direction of the bottom of the wave face by changing your balance on to the rear foot. The difference to the previously described top turn is that you continue

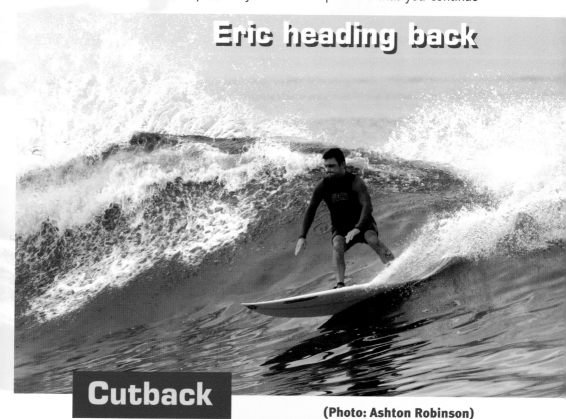

Eric heading back

Cutback

(Photo: Ashton Robinson)

turning by keeping the pressure on the rear foot and thereby on the tail of the board until the nose of the board is pointing in the opposite direction to the breaking direction of the wave (the direction you were surfing in beforehand). This means you are now riding back to the more powerful part of the wave. Cutback!

But wait a minute, now the white water is coming full steam towards you. Simply either do another turn back into the 'correct' direction before the approaching foam reaches you, or you can use the power of this foam to drive you in the original direction again. If you make a turn directly on or with the foam (turning down the wave face), this will automatically drive you in the right direction. This latter move is called a 'rebound'. Of course, this is not an easy manoeuvre, but the rolling foam conveniently offers itself as a springboard to go back in the right direction. Executed well, this is a spectacular move. The rebound, done in one flowing move with the cutback, mentioned earlier, is called a 'roundhouse cutback'. We will look at this a little closer in the chapter for the advanced.

Surfing Backhand

Actually, this is not a manoeuvre in itself. Despite this, it is something that has to be constantly practiced in order to master it. It feels a bit strange at first, but the more you practice it the more surfing backhand becomes natural. There are two main difficulties. First of all you are surfing with your back to the wave. You can hardly see what is happening behind you. In addition, to see what is happening to the wave behind you at all, you have to twist your neck and look over your shoulder. Having to keep turning your head makes it more difficult to keep your balance. In addition, weighting and unweighting your board seems not to be so easy. Only practice will help. Here are a few tips before you try all the manoeuvres we covered earlier on your backhand.

During a bottom turn you should make sure that your forward hand (goofy – right; regular – left) is stretched out, pointing towards the wave face. The forward hand towards the wave face? How? What do you mean? Just imagine that you would try to prevent your bottom from touching the water by supporting yourself on your forward hand as you lean into the turn. This would of course be not in front of the body but behind it. This stance helps you to balance your body and to transfer your speed in the right direction. During the bottom turn your weight is on your heels, and at the moment you turn, your knees are fully bent. You are looking over your shoulder and focus on the point where your turn will take you. Your forward foot should be in an angle to the nose of the board – regulars around 2 o'clock and goofys around 10 o'clock (– the nose of your board is at 12 o'clock).

The top turn comes a little easier if you shift your centre of mass relatively hard towards the bottom of the wave face. To start with, you can simply try to push your bottom outwards as you turn. At the same time you push your rear foot towards the top of the wave. This gives the board a turning momentum.

Backside Top Turn

(Photo: Bill Morris, O'Neill)

To do a cutback you really only have to do a forehand turn (almost like a bottom turn on the wave face) in the opposite direction. With your face looking towards the bottom of the wave you make a turn against the breaking direction. The weighting is the same as the forehand bottom turn. Weight is on the toes, with the rear hand stretched in the direction of the water (– in front of the body), and your body leaning into the turn. Try to imagine that you are actually doing a forehand turn. This way the manoeuvre will almost seem like the easiest backside manoeuvre of all.

To practice surfing on your backhand, a 'point break' is the best spot because the wave only breaks in one direction. You are automatically forced to surf backhand (– for goofys a right wave, and for regulars a left one). If there are only beach breaks, use one of your sessions to practice only backhand. Stick to it, and do not fall back into surfing on your forehand until you have got it wired.

3.3 General Tips for the Beginner

- At the beginning keep away from other water sportsmen.

- Never surf alone or without supervision.

- Watch the waves rather one time too many before you enter the water.

- Give it everything when paddling for a wave plus two extra strokes – even when you believe that you have already caught the wave.

- If you are underwater, count until you surface again. This takes away your fear because generally you are only held underwater for a few seconds.

- If everything gets a bit too much for you, go back to the beach with the next wave riding in the prone position.

- Watch out for the shore break!

- Weight on the tail of the board reduces speed, and weighting the front increases it.

- To surf along a wave, paddle for the wave at an angle.

- **Never give up! And, above all never give up!**

ADVANCED SURFING

By now, you will have surfed a few waves, and will have gone through the full washing cycle a few times. You will have sometimes thought that your last moment had come while you were scratching over a big set of waves and, you will certainly know that one of the worst feelings in this sport is putting on a cold and wet rashguard. You are sitting at home and can think of nothing else but the unbelievable feeling of gliding on a wave. You sit there planning your next surfing trip and places like Hawaii, Australia or Bali are buzzing around in your head. Ah well, obviously you have a severe case of surf fever and you simply cannot shake it off. You better start thinking about how you are going to explain to your girl- or boyfriend that, in the future, there will only be holidays in places that have waves.

In the next chapter we want to go into a few things to do with advanced equipment, describe some manoeuvres for the advanced, give a few tips about how to behave when you are surfing with other surfers in the water, and talk a little about the weather, waves and different sea bottoms.

1 What's Next?

So you think you are an advanced surfer, you have skipped the first pages and started reading this book here. But who can actually call himself an advanced surfer?

Is it the surfer who surfs the Hawaiian winter monster waves, or perhaps the one who knows how to tie a leash to a surfboard? It is difficult to say who is and who is not. Therefore, we have tried to compile a few basic requirements that you should at least have before we move on.

Give me more!

(Photo: Bill Morris, O'Neill)

1.1 Requirements for an Advanced Surfer

The first thing is that you should be a very good swimmer, above all in the ocean. Splashing around in a swimming pool is one thing, but getting back to the beach, swimming between currents and waves after you have snapped your leash, is a completely different story. You should always be able to swim from the line-up back to the beach. A further important requirement is the ability to 'read' the waves, so that you can at least tell whether the waves are surfable or not. It is also very important to be able to recognise, from the beach, possible currents as well as other potential hazards such as shallow water over reef, rocks, etc. In addition, you should know something about the sort of bottom the waves break on – for example, whether the bottom is sand or a reef. Attached to this is the ability to judge the size of the waves. This is extremely difficult when there is no other surfer in the water, and you have nothing else to compare the size of the wave with. Viewing from the beach, the waves always appear smaller than when you are out there amongst them.

It is even more difficult to assess who is an advanced surfer and who is not. There are, of course, different opinions about this. Again let's try to find a few basics. An advanced surfer knows how to paddle well i.e., he knows how to lie on the board, and how to catch a wave by paddling with the necessary speed so that the wave actually picks him up. Standing up should not present a challenge any more, and he should be able to surf the unbroken part of a wave diagonally. He should be able to manage and to control the manoeuvres we described in the previous chapter. Let's make this clear – the surfboard should go where you want it to go and not vice versa.

However, all these are only the basics – you should not be tempted to think, "No problem, I've stood up four times in a row without nose diving, I must be what those guys call advanced" – and off you go to surf Uluwatu in Bali. Being able to judge your own ability in respect of the conditions at any given break is surely also a factor defining an advanced surfer.

1.2 Equipment for the Advanced

Let's start with the surfboard. There are all types and sizes of surfboards, and many waves call for particular boards to ride them successfully. Big waves need different boards than small waves. Hollow breaking waves call for a different board than those used for flat, mellow rolling waves, and there are different boards for fast breaking waves and slow breaking waves. But let's not get carried away, and since we are not all pro surfers, whose boards are paid for by sponsors, and who carry giant boardbags stuffed with at least ten or so boards everywhere they go, let us limit this to the basic shapes. Essentially a surfer needs two types of boards – a shortboard for small to medium sized waves and a semi-gun for more serious ones. These two types of boards will be described in the next section and should be your base quiver.

(Photo: Bill Morris, O'Neill)

All right, now go and put that old log (we mean your beginner's board) away and jump on a smaller, more manoeuvrable board called a shortboard. Unless you want to carry on your career as a longboarder which is OK too, but not the focus of this book.

A shortboard is between 6 and 7 foot long, approximately 16–19 inches wide, and between 2 and 3 inches thick. The selection of the right board depends on your size, your weight, your ability and, last but not least, the kind of waves that you are going to use it in. For young people, according to age, size and weight,

Longboarders charge, too!

boards between 5'5" and 6'8" are the most common. A grown-up needs a board between 6'1" and 6'10". Heavier and larger surfers should use a slightly longer and thicker board. As an example let's consider a surfer who is about 185 cm tall and weighs around 75-80 kilos. For this surfer, a shortboard upwards from 6'3", about 2.5 inches thick and around about 18 inches wide would be the best option. Please do not take these figures as firm measurements. Even among the pro surfers you will find dramatic differences based on individual preferences. This said, the right board obviously also depends on your level of skill. Someone who is just moving up from the beginner status will find that with a small, thin board and its inherent low buoyancy, paddling will be made unnecessarily more difficult, and he will often not reach the necessary speed and miss many waves. In summary, thicker and longer boards, just like the beginner's board, allow easier paddling and make it easier to catch waves because they float better. Shorter, thinner boards are generally more manoeuvrable and are easy to duck-dive with. The bottom line is that it is up to each surfer to find out what works best for him by trying many different sizes and shapes (borrow boards from friends and rent them from shops). Also talking to the board shapers will help you understand how different designs influence the performance of a board.

Shortboards work best in small to medium sized waves. Because of their shape and weight they guarantee maximum manoeuvrability (and fun). However, every surfer should have a secret love affair – the semi-gun. Simply looking at a semi-gun will trigger daydreams of powerful groundswells, adrenaline surges as the horizon grows darker and giant sets roll in. If only you could take your semi-gun to

Shortboards

**Shortboards with square tail,
swallow tail and semi-gun with pintail
(Photo: Sigi Opitz, Ineika Funcenter)**

bed with you every night (we do know a few funny stories though). OK, OK, enough of this – but what is a semi-gun? It is a long, narrow board that is mainly used for surfing in large and/or hollow waves. Its size is between 6'10 to 8 feet for a semi gun and up to 10 feet for a fully fledged Hawaiian gun. It is approximately 17.5 to 20 inches wide and between 2.25 and 3.75 inches thick.

On the one hand, the length allows the surfer to catch large and steep waves more easily, and on the other hand, it provides him with the necessary stability needed when surfing at a higher speed and helps him to cope with often-larger chops on the face of some bigger waves. The thickness of the board additionally supports this. Do not think that larger and/or steeper waves would be easier to catch; It is quite the opposite. Especially here, because of the higher speed at which the waves are travelling you have to paddle extremely hard to catch the wave. Bigger boards simply paddle faster. More about this later. Another important point is the confidence a gun gives in large waves. You can trust your gun that it will guide you down the biggest waves you have ever surfed and bring you safely back to the beach. Therefore, the gun is not only a surfing tool but also a psychological tool to master powerful waves as it will put you in the right state of mind for conquering the big stuff. It is not simply an extended shortboard. Generally, there are two sorts of shapes. The full on gun shaped to surf the classic Big-Wave style: take-off, straight drop down the face without wiping-out and a long stretched out bottom turn. Modern shaped semi guns are narrower and thinner giving the board additional manoeuvrability. A modern shaped semi gun is exactly the right choice for an average to good surfer.

Most of today's semi guns have a so-called "pintail" i.e., it tapers to a point at the end of the board. How pointed a pintail should be, depends on the waves where it will be

Hawaiian Gun
(Photo: Menges & Diel)

ridden. For example, in Hawaii, some people who surf at Waimea Bay and Sunset Beach (both are places on the North Shore of the island of Oahu), use extremely pointed pintails, so that both ends of the board often look almost identically pointed. Sometimes the tail is even more pointed than the nose. A board like this, however, will only go straight. These big guns are also called "rhino chasers". It all goes back to a remark made by Big-Wave legend Pat Curren (Tom Curren's father), who said something like: "You do not go hunting rhinos with a BB gun. If you're going to hunt big waves take a big gun." The length of a gun depends on where it is going to be used. Rhino chasers, about 10 feet long, are used for waves in places such as Waimea and Sunset (Hawaii), Todos Santos (Baja California, Mexico) or Mavericks (California). In Europe, even the most daring will hardly need a gun over 8 feet. So, as you can see, there are endless different shapes and lengths of shortboards and guns. When you buy a board, you should watch out for the following design variations. Tail, rocker, rails, stringer etc. So let's take a closer look.

Tail: The term tail refers to the rear end of the surfboard. Today's shortboards essentially use two types of tails. One is called the "square tail". It almost appears as if it has been squarely cut off at the end. According to how rounded the two corners are, it is also called a "rounded square tail". A board with a square tail is very responsive and is therefore best suited for radical manoeuvres in small waves. If you will mainly be surfing beachbreaks, you should get a board with a square tail. Please do not misunderstand us. We have experienced beachbreak waves in France (e.g., in Hossegor) that could take on many waves seen in Hawaii (of course on an "off" day). However, overall, you will find small to medium-sized waves on the average beachbreak in France, California or elsewhere ranging from 2 to 6 foot. Just the perfect size to have a bit of fun. A board with a square tail will be the right choice here.

The other popular type of tail is called a "pintail" which we have already mentioned in the context of semi-guns. Similarly, to the square tail, a pintail that has been rounded off is called just that – a "rounded pintail". The pintail is mostly used in connection with the gun shapes. This said, pintails are making a bit of a comeback on short boards also. Pintails work best in fast, hollow waves in the 4-6 foot range, like those found for example at the Superbank (Queensland, Australia) or Mundacca (in the Basque country, Northern Spain).

A pintail is somewhat more difficult to turn, but has the advantage of giving the board more stability when surfing at higher speed. The tail does not break away as easily as it cuts deeper into the water.

Finally, perhaps the "swallow tail" is worth a mention. It literally looks like the tail of a swallow at the rear. The shapers used this type of tail a lot in the 1970s, and today is often found in specific shaped boards e.g., the so-called "fish" used for getting extra flotation (and fun) in small, powerless waves (or big 8 foot Sumatra if you are Tom Curren)

Fins: Most modern shortboards and guns have three fins, and are called a "thruster". The thruster was invented by Australian Simon Anderson in 1980. The two outside fins are positioned approximately 1 foot from the tail of the board and about 1 inch in from the rails. The third fin is placed directly in the middle of the board and is about 4 inches away from the tail. The advantage of the thruster is that one fin always remains in the water, even during a radical carve on the rail. As a result, the tail will not break away (unless you do a tail slide manoeuvre on purpose). The thruster makes it possible to gain additional acceleration coming out of fast turns such as, for example, the bottom turn. There are also boards with other fin constellations. As an example, a single fin is sometimes used on a gun

Thruster

with rounded square tail, hard rails and removable fins (Photo: Menges & Diel)

with a very pointed pintail. As we have mentioned before these boards are used for steep, very fast waves. Boards with two (made famous by four-time world champion Mark Richards) or four fins (called a "quad") are not seen so much these days. Very practical, particularly while you are travelling, are fin systems that allow you to remove the fins. Those, who have ever experienced the misery of unpacking their boards after a flight with perfect waves waiting just outside the front door – only to find the fins broken off, have particularly welcomed the introduction of these systems. They not only provide safer travelling for your board but also allow you to change and experiment with different fin shapes.

You must still take care when putting in and taking off the fins from the board. It is very easy to damage the board when trying to force a fin in or out of its slot. Several different systems have been developed but are far away from being perfect. As every system has its pros and cons, it is best that you choose the system with which you personally feel most comfortable. You should always watch for new developments and improvements in this area as well.

Rail: The surfboard's rails are defined by the degree of their rounded edges. 'Soft', smoothly shaped rails, running from the upper side to the bottom, are well suitable for the beginner. A board with soft rails is easy to turn. Advanced surfers, however, would be better off choosing a board with 'hard' rails. The edges are smoothly rounded off on the upper side and at the bottom there are clearly defined edges. These dig deep into the water and thereby give a better grip on the wave than the soft rails. They have an advantage on steep wave faces when, after the take-off, the edge digs into the water and despite the steepness the board maintains a good grip. With soft rails there is always a danger that the board will break away and slip sideways. This is a similar effect to skiing with badly honed edges on your skis.

Rocker: The term 'rocker' describes the surfboard's bottom longitudinal curve, from the tail to the nose. However, often only the curve at the nose – the so-called 'nose lift' – is what is meant. Generally speaking, most shortboards and guns should have a lifted-up nose. This is determined by the form of the more hollow breaking waves which usually have somewhat of an edge at the bottom. If the nose of the board did not have the lift, then the tip would always dig straight into the water at this edge. Furthermore, the more overall rocker the board has the more the board gains in manoeuvrability. If the rocker is too fierce, the board will push water in front of it and slow you down. Different surfers prefer different shapes of rockers. If possible, you should try out the different rocker-shapes to see which one suit you best.

Stringer: The stringer is a thin strip of wood that runs down the centre of the board. This gives the board its core strength and rigidity and lessens the danger of it breaking. Guns often have a thicker stringer than shortboards because they are exposed to stronger forces in bigger waves.

Despite the fact that the stringer is only rather thin, it gives the necessary strength. If it is damaged or split anywhere along its length, the board will be extremely unstable, and it will probably break in half the next time you stand on it. You should make sure that the stringer is undamaged when you are buying a board.

These are some of the more important terms used, and are those that you will need when buying a board. Before you buy a board pick it up under the arm. Look down it from tail to front to see its rocker and overall curve. You must get the feel of its shape and rails. This will tell you whether this board is the right one for you or not. You can also have one made especially for you. This is a so-called 'custom-made board'. However, this may take some time to get shaped and depends on the shaper and his workload. Let's say you want a genuine Rusty Preisendorfer, Glenn Minami or a Phil Byrne, then you might have to invest at least a few weeks in a very special board.

If you use a relatively unknown shaper then it will usually be much quicker. The big advantage of custom-made boards is that the board will be made exactly to your own requirements. You can tell the shaper what your surfing ability is (being truthful here really pays off), and where you want to use the board. If you are able to, you can tell him your preferences for thickness, width and length, as well as the kind of tail and rocker. Last but not least, you can choose your own colours and graphics.

For the advanced surfer, the following accessories should also get a mention:

Grip deck: A grip deck or pad is glued on to the surfboard to give the surfer a good grip on his board without using wax. There are grip decks for the tail and rear foot only as well as so-called 'full decks' for rear and front foot, which however have really come out of fashion over the last years. Some decks have a slight rise on the tail pad, called a 'kick'. This allows the surfer to apply even more pressure on the tail, and prevents the foot from slipping off the back of the board during radical manoeuvres. There are a number of different decks on the market that are recommended by the various pro surfers. It is difficult to say which the best is. One of the disadvantages with almost all the decks, however, is that when you are surfing with surf boots (e.g. over reefs in the tropics), sometimes you feel as if your feet are glued to the board as well. It is then difficult to adjust your foot position while surfing.

Helmet: Surfers use a helmet mainly when the waves break over a reef or rocks in extremely shallow water. A helmet can also offer some protection against the sun. There are helmets with and without a visor. The visor is good to protect the eyes against the glaring sun while you sit out in the line-up waiting for waves. A particular pro surfer from Hawaii even had the nerve to drop into a wave with the visor up and then pull it down before the wave started tubing. He claimed he could see clearer while in the tube. We apologize for not being able to prove his claim ourselves.

Finally, a mention of the leash and boots. A normal leash for a shortboard is about 4-6 feet long. For a gun you should buy a longer leash, about 8 feet long. In large waves the leash is subjected to a greater strain, and therefore has to be stronger and longer. The fastening mechanism of your leash is also critical. If the leash is caught up on a rock or is stuck between coral, you must be able to undo it with one rapid movement. You should practice on land how to quickly remove your leash because if you are stuck underwater after a wipe-out, every second will count and you will not have time to start thinking which way or the other you should open the leash. Many leashes these days have a little flap on the velcro strap that wraps around your ankle and opens the leash in one pull. When we were in Hawaii many years ago, and we asked the local behind the counter what the little flap was for, he looked at us with a big smile, pulled it open and said, "'Cos you don't die." So have a good look at your leash before you put it on.

You should have at least one pair of surf boots, even if you do not intend to surf in ice-cold water where they are essential to keep your feet warm. They will also protect you from reefs and sea urchins. On some beaches you have to walk across a reef to get to the water. Without boots, this is nearly impossible. Just watch surfers in Bali, they wear nothing but shorts and boots to avoid reefcuts exiting and entering the water at low tide. The soles of the shoes should not be as thick as the rubber on diving shoes or those used by windsurfers, as you would lose the feel for the board.

1.3 The Surf Code

Those of you, who do not have their own private wave directly in front of their front door must learn the surf code and a few unwritten rules by heart, before paddling out between other surfers somewhere in the world. First of all the most important of all the rules – the right of way. Basically the surfer who is on the inside, nearest to the point where the wave is breaking (the white water), has the right of way. A surfer who takes-off into a wave, but is further away from another surfer who has already started closer to the break and has started at the same time, has to kick out and leave the wave. To interfere with the right of way of another surfer is called a 'drop-in' and a simple DON'T. The surfer, about to start must always make sure there is no one taking-off on the inside. Besides the resulting arguments, drop-ins are often the cause of injuries or

Sorry, buddy!

**The surfer on the left, riding closer to the curl has priority
and is being dropped in on by the other surfer. Don't drop in!
(Photo: Menges/Diel)**

damaged boards. One exception to this rule is when a surfer has caught a wave further out and is surfing past a surfer waiting to catch a wave. If the waiting surfer, who is now practically behind the other, starts into the wave, so to say from behind, he is actually nearer to the breaking point of the wave and thus theoretically would have the right of way. In this case however, the surfer who stood up first has the right of way. This often leads to disagreements in the water.

A further important rule is that the surfer who is riding a wave has the right of way over another surfer paddling out. This means that in some cases the one paddling out must actually paddle into the white water (and receive a thrashing) instead of safely going over the shoulder of the wave as this is also where the one riding the wave is aiming at. This can be quite tough especially in bigger waves. Who would not want to slip over the shoulder of a big incoming wave and not have the next one break on top of him? Let's summarise this:

- **The surfer who is already up and riding on a wave or who is closer to the breaking point of the wave on the take-off has absolute priority.**
- **Someone surfing has priority over someone paddling out.**

Now a few words about the unwritten rules. If you are paddling out and a broken wave is coming towards you, do not throw your board away and bail out but always hold on to your board and at least try to duck-dive through – that is unless you really fear for your life as a monster wave is breaking right on top of you. If you let your board go, the surfer behind you, who gets your board smashed into his face, or the one surfing the wave, who may collide with your loose board, will not exactly become your best friend. Equally, something you should avoid is to let go of your board or even push your board off in front of you into the wave if you have to abort your take-off for whatever reason. If there is a surfer already on the wave, he will get the board straight onto his head.

If you are surfing on a beach where the waves are breaking left and right (a so-called peak), you should call out "left" or "right" to any other surfer about to start at the same time as yourself, to indicate to him which way you want to go. Otherwise the person going right and the person going left will no doubt meet (collide) somewhere in the middle.

Something that always creates a bad atmosphere, and is sure to raise the anger of not only the hardcore locals, is when a surfer constantly tries to paddle on the inside to get priority even after he has just entered the line-up or paddled back

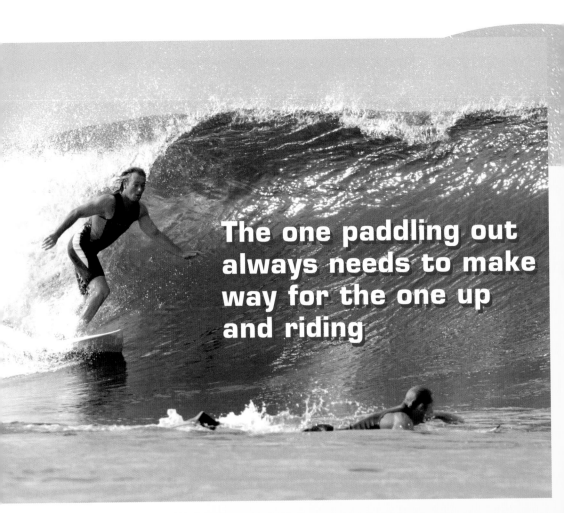

The one paddling out always needs to make way for the one up and riding

(Photo: Ashton Robinson)

out after catching a wave. Another unpopular behaviour is called "snaking". Imagine you are sitting out in the water waiting for a wave. The surfer next to you is sitting actually closer to the anticipated point of the wave breaking (he is sitting on your inside and has priority). When the wave rolls in, you quickly paddle around him to get on his inside and gain priority, or even worse, paddle right in front of him so that he cannot paddle for the wave. Do this to a local in Hawaii and you will find out quite a different (unpleasant) interpretation of the Aloha spirit.

This brings us straight to one of the most important unwritten rules that is to respect the locals at any surfbreak around the world. Remember they have been surfing there every day for years. You cannot simply show up there one day and expect to get all the best waves of the day. Localism has figured as a much-discussed topic in surfing magazines for many years. You might have read about fights in the water, broken surfboards, cars being broken into etc. On La Réunion (Indian Ocean), we once saw a boogie-boarder draw a knife and attack an Australian surfer because he had dropped in on him. Certain beaches in California or the Westside of Oahu (Hawaii) are well renowned for heavy localism. Most of the time the arguments start because a surfer shows disrespect for the unwritten rules and/or for the locals. Respect simply means to leave some waves for the locals (sometimes even without attempting to paddle for them), await your turn for the inside, do not paddle straight to the inside when you paddle out, and of course never drop in!

However, to put a few things in perspective: naturally, you should not just sit there and let everyone go past you out of sheer politeness. Use your skills and try hard to catch a wave. Do not insist on your right of way and never fight (against another surfer) for a wave. Nothing looks more ridiculous than seeing two people trying to fight in the water, and half drowning themselves in the process. Another important rule to avoid trouble in the water is quite simple. Don't be an idiot! That is the best way to express this, because there are some surfers who think they can do anything and everything without having to worry about the other surfers in the water. These people simply attract trouble! Apart from this, a good surfer should not need to steal waves from others the dirty way (e.g. snaking!), because he will catch enough waves anyway by using his paddling and positioning skills.

All this said, localism is not as bad and ever-present as it sometimes sounds. We, personally, have never had any serious issues with any of the locals we encountered around the world apart of course from the odd little abuse.

1.4 The Duck-dive

Yes, the duck-dive indeed! Probably, this is one of the most important things that you have to master, otherwise you will never get out over the white water and into the real line-up on any of the bigger days. If you have seen the movie "North Shore", then you will probably know what you have to do. In case you have not, then write this down: "You have to dive like a duck if you want to surf on the North Shore". Sounds a bit cheesy and you do not have to duck-dive along most of the North Shore anyway to get out, as most breaks have deep channels to paddle through. However, there is some truth in the matter. Duck diving essentially means to dive under a wave with your board still under you. The critical bit is obviously to get your highly buoyant board under water deep enough with you, so that a wave can pass over you without throwing you back and around too much. When you push your board down (with your foot or knee) your bottom will naturally be the last part of your body sticking out from the water for a split second. This actually does resemble the movements of a real duck diving down.

One of the secrets of duck-diving is paddling speed. The individual sequence of movements can be described as follows. A wave, that has already broken, or is about to break, is rolling towards you. You paddle up to it at full speed. At the last moment when the white water or the wave is about to hit, you press the front half of the board under water, by doing a kind of a press-up. The wave is now right over you, but the rear half is still out of the water. Now you press the tail down with your knee or your foot. You will have to try this out to discover whether you find it easier with the knee or the foot. You can actually press down harder and further with your foot, thus pushing the board deeper under the surface of the water. Using your foot will give you an advantage in larger waves.

You can use your other leg to balance out the turbulences almost like a rudder when you are underwater. For a short moment, your whole body and your board are now under the water, before natural flotation will push you and your board up again. The speed reached in paddling gives you the necessary forward momentum to dive through the wave. On the other side you bob up like a cork because of the strong buoyancy of your board. It is important that the duck-dive is carried out in one flowing motion. Pushing the front and the tail down should happen quickly one after the other in the same movement. You have to time the duck-dive in such a way that both you and the board go under just at the moment where the wave or white water reaches you. As the wave passes over you, give your board some extra forward movement against the pull of the turbulence by fully extending your arms and pushing forward. Because of the board's natural buoyancy you will only be able to dive for a short time; thus timing is of vital importance. The more volume your board has the more difficult the duck-dive will be.

Tip: Keep your eyes open in clear water so that you can see the wave and turbulence passing over you. This way you can get a feeling for when you have to stop fighting and surface again. A good deep duck-dive is difficult and requires a lot of

The sequence of the duck-dive:

- **Paddle strongly towards the wave or the white water**

- **Shortly before the wave hits you, push the nose of the board deep down into the water with both hands.**

- **Directly afterwards push the tail under the water with the foot or the knee.**

- **Under water, give the board a push forward with your arms.**

- **Surface and straight away begin to paddle (the next wave is already waiting).**

(Drawings: Stefan "Muli" Müller)

practice. There are some surfers, who even after several years still have not managed to master it. As a result they get pushed back and lose a lot of ground and power every time they are not able to duck-dive under an incoming set. So, keep working on your duck-diving techniques and you will surf more efficiently and become less afraid of clean up wave sets that roll though the line-up.

2 How waves are created?

No doubt, waves are the most important thing that a surfer needs. They are the reason why he keeps travelling round the world hoping to find, somewhere, the perfect wave. A surfer has to know how and why waves are created, where they come from and in which direction they spread out. He has to understand how the moon and the tide influence the waves, and how a sandbank, reef or submerged rocks affect the way in which the waves break. Being able to read a weather map helps the surfer to recognise a possible swell. Of course, you can use online surf reports, with weather forecasts and predictions on wave heights, as well as live pictures of surfing spots around the world. Nevertheless, every surfer should know what those circles on the weather map are all about.

Naturally, we are not going to hold a lecture on weather forecasts here, and it is almost certain that the next chapter will be somewhat dry reading. However, we think that every surfer should have at least some basic knowledge of the connection between weather and waves.

2.1 Weather

What do all the circles and figures mean on the weather chart? Why does a depression or a low bring waves and a high-pressure zone usually does not?

The sun's rays heat up the earth. Layers of air are warmed up and rise. Colder air streams in to take their place. The rotation of the earth moves the air around and airstreams are created.

When warm airstreams meet cold ones turbulence occurs. The cold airstream pushes itself under the warm one and heat and energy is released with the result that clouds and air circulate. This is how a storm begins, circulating counter-clockwise in the Northern Hemisphere, and clockwise in the Southern Hemisphere. The lines and circles on the weather chart are so-called "isobars". These define areas with the same air pressure and are measured in millibars.

The numbers that are usually written next to the isobars tell you how high or how low the pressure is in the particular area. They are measured in relation to sea level. Wind is created when the airstreams from a depression, and a high-pressure area, equal each other out. The direction of the airstreams flows from the area of high pressure to areas of low pressure.

The surfer's favourite picture of the weather chart is a depression where the isobars are close to each other and under 1,000 millibars in the centre of it. Such a depression will bring waves if it is sitting or moving in the right direction. The best waves are created by tropical storms such as cyclones, typhoons or hurricanes – basically these are all terms for one and the same thing: a storm depression. However you want to call them, one thing is for sure – they create waves. In order to produce surfable waves these storms must stay centred far off shore otherwise they obviously become a threat.

There are numerous weather conditions in the world that can produce a good swell. However, it would be well beyond the scope of this book to cover the ideal weather situations on the entire world's seas; you would probably fall asleep anyway.

"Tunnel vision"

(Photo: Smico, Kelly Smith)

At this point let's take a short look at the subject of winds near the coastline. Generally, one can say that the wind close to the coastline will blow in the direction of the warmer area. During the day, the sun warms up the land to such a degree that the wind will blow from the sea to cool it down – a so-called "onshore". During the night, the land slowly cools down and the wind backs round to blow in the direction of the warmer sea. This is why most beaches have an "offshore" wind early in the morning. This wind usually turns round at about midday. The offshore blows against the waves slowing them down but smoothing the surface. Thus, the wave will break cleaner and with more perfection. This said, a strong offshore wind would often make paddling for a wave more difficult.

You will have to give at least a couple or so extra strokes if you want to catch it. Sometimes you will hardly be able to see the wave when you are trying to take-

Ideal weather conditions for perfect waves on the French Atlantic coast. Start packing your boards!

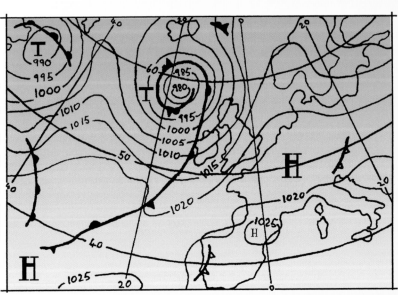

(Drawing: Menges & Diel)

off because of all the spray created by the offshore wind. However, the extra effort is definitely worth the effort in offshore winds. Contrary to this, an onshore wind causes the waves to break earlier and the surface of the water will be choppy. Both not ideal for surfing. Strong onshore winds usually make the surf unrideable. The ideal wind condition is however, waves with no wind at all. Certain weather constellations can create this dream-like scenario. The water surface is then nice and smooth. These conditions are called "glassy". If you are lucky, perfect conditions are sometimes met when, just before the wind turns from off to onshore or vice versa, there is a stillness with no wind at all. Therefore, always remember the old saying the early bird catches the 'tube' or something like that anyway! The morning session – dawn patrol – is therefore often the best session of the whole day.

(Photo: Ashton Robinson)

Just perfect!

4 foot and glassy

The Life-cycle of a Wave

Waves are produced by storms far out at sea. Water is set in motion by a storm. When the surface begins to ripple and becomes turbulent, it is called "chop" or "wind chop". If the wind keeps blowing the chop gets larger and larger and gradually a swell is formed. At the beginning the waves, whipped up by the storm, are unstructured and move in all directions. A real swell is formed when the wind blows in the same direction for a sustained period of time and the chops on the water surface turn into a structured swell. The swell then begins to move towards the coast. Such a swell is often referred to as a "groundswell". The waves often travel thousands of kilometres. When they break on a beach they will have lost some height and the gap between the waves will be longer or shorter, depending on how far the waves have travelled. Generally, big waves move faster than small ones and therefore when waves travel over the ocean they group themselves into sets of bigger and sets of smaller waves depending on their travelling speed. This is why they also arrive in the surf line-up as bigger and smaller sets i.e., groups of 3-9 waves at once. A pause, a so-called lull, follows each set. Again, this lull can be longer or shorter depending on the strength and the so-called wave period of the swell. These lulls are important as it gives surfers a chance to paddle out between sets. The type of swell that every surfer prays for is created by a groundswell, where the waves come in regular groups, with no wind blowing as they break onto the beach. Quite the opposite is a so-called "windswell". The water is churned up by strong winds near the coast and the ocean often looks as if someone had dumped a ton or two of washing detergent in it. Further out to sea the surface is covered with white crests. These conditions are called "blown out" (too much wind), and unfortunately happen far too often.

The Tide

The tide also plays an important role in the formation of waves. Tide is the product of the simultaneous force of attraction of the sun and the moon, as well as the gravitational pull of the earth. Tides are either called a low tide (shallow water) or a high tide (deep water).

Low tide and high tide change on a six hourly rhythm and make a time jump of about an hour each day. A useful aid to the surfer are tide tables or tide charts for each beach or the whole coastline. These will tell you exactly the time of low or high tide. The tables also give you coefficients for each day expressing the difference between the low and high tide. Surfers look for so-called "King tides", which are tides with extreme differences between high and low tide, and have very high coefficients. Tide charts can usually be found in the local surf shop. If there are no surf shops around you can often find tide charts in the local newspaper as they are also used by boats and ships. You can also ask the local fishermen. They usually know best.

Low and high tides have a great influence on a surf spot. If a swell is building, the waves will often get larger with the incoming high tide. The opposite occurs with an outgoing low tide where the waves may get smaller but generally steeper as they will break in shallower water. This is, of course, all very dependent on the type of beach. Every surf spot has an ideal tide constellation for it to break well. This can be incoming tide, mid- tide, high or low tide. You should therefore always know whether the tide is going out or coming in. At some surf spots not knowing the tide can be dangerous. For example, waves breaking over a reef, which can normally be surfed without problems during a high tide, will be steeper during low tide, yet will be breaking in shallow receding water (if there is any left at all). A wipe-out in the shallows over a razor-sharp reef can cause nasty injuries. In the Cook Islands in the South Pacific, for example, you surf only on the incoming high tide. The waves break in passages or breaks in the coral reef, which encircle the island. At low tide the water from the lagoons inside the ring of the coral reef is sucked out through these passages. It can be almost impossible to get back through these passages, as the outgoing current can be very strong. Riding a wave over the almost dry reef is often the only solution to get yourself back in to the inside of the lagoon. However, you would not do your surfboard any favours and you may end up with a reef cut or two yourself.

2.2   How to Read a Surf Spot

You know the story. "Come on, these waves are no good, let's go back to the other beach. The waves are much better there – Or wait a minute, look at that set coming in, let's stay here! ...and so on and so forth. We are talking about the surf check. It belongs to surfing just like paddling does. Many non-surfers often do not understand why it so important to just look at the waves for a few moments, check out a few different spots before you make a call where to go out and simply do a surf check. Knowledge of the surf spot, its bottom and the currents, can be the deciding factor between fun and frustration. Learn to 'read' the surf spot. "Let's paddle out, and then have a look" can often end up with an

"Surf check"

Sunset Beach, Hawaii (Photo: Ecki Hillebrecht)

unpleasant surprise. Naturally, a surf check on a beach break is not as critical as on a reef in Indonesia. Nevertheless, beach breaks can have their own obstacles in the form of strong currents between the sandbanks, and tricky shore breaks.

Let us take a look at some of the different types of bottoms and the influence these have on how a wave breaks. On all beaches waves meet the bottom of the ocean, and push their energy up in the direction of its crest, causing them to break. The way the waves now break depends largely on the bottom and its shape, and that is what we are now going to have a closer look at.

The Beach Break

The "beach break" is the simplest and least dangerous form of a surf break. The bottom consists of sand, which more or less gradually rises underwater. The wave breaks either on an offshore sandbank (100 meteres or so from the beach) or directly onto the beach.

Best for surfing are the beaches where the waves break on offshore sandbanks. The best sandbanks are often found near stone piers, rivermouths or harbour walls, but of course they can also be found on open beaches. Sandbanks are usually surrounded by currents. On open beaches a current runs parallel between the beach and the sandbank. Strong currents between sandbanks eventually run back out to sea through deepwater channels between sandbanks. The currents in these channels are proportionally stronger the narrower they are. The surfer can use these currents almost as a conveyor to carry him out to the line-up with sometimes very little effort. They key is to spot the current from the beach before you paddle out. Near to harbour walls or piers the current often runs out directly along the side of these. While paddling out close to something like a rock pier in bigger surf can be a somewhat intimidating experience, it is often the easiest and sometimes only way out.

A beach break usually provides a simple, short ride. The waves roll softly towards the beach. A common view at beach breaks is that the wave breaks along its whole length at once, this is called a "close-out", and often a take-off is all you will get before the wave closes down. The biggest disadvantage of beach breaks is their unpredictability – i.e., the line-up is often not clearly defined and it is hard to tell where the waves will actually break. Another drawback is the often insurmountable mass of white water that you have to duck-dive through to get out, as well as the increasing number of close-out waves as the swell gets bigger.

Nevertheless, not all beach breaks gently roll off as described above. There are also breaks which literally suck up the water from the sandbanks creating intense tubes. These waves break top-to-bottom, i.e., the lip of the wave breaks directly into the base of the wave. Typically, reef waves break top-to-bottom. There are, however, several world-class waves that break onto a sandy bottom and have this top-to-bottom characteristic. Puerto Escondido in Mexico – the Mexican pipeline – is an example. The sand is so hard there that the waves break onto it as if on a reef. Other world class beach breaks that can deliver serious tubes (and poundings) are Hossegor (France), Duranbah (Australia) – and pretty much every beach break around the world on its particular day when everything falls into place and for a day or so your average beach break is "all time".

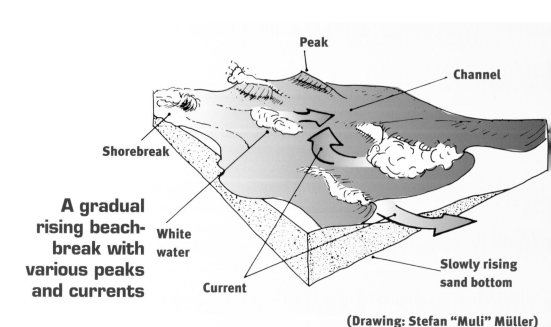

A gradual rising beach-break with various peaks and currents

Peak

Channel

Shorebreak

White water

Current

Slowly rising sand bottom

(Drawing: Stefan "Muli" Müller)

Reef Break

The most spectacular and beautiful waves in the world break on reefs. The depth of the water varies to extremes. The wave often breaks quite far from shore, but in spite of this, the waves break in dangerously shallow water. Some reefs rise up steeply underwater, so the swell hits it without being slowed down by a gradually rising ocean floor. The result is that the wave's energy is quickly transformed into height and the wave stands up almost like a wall out of the water. Sometimes it appears as if there is hardly any swell, and suddenly a steep green wall stands up in front of you. On reefs, waves usually break steep, hollow and top-to-bottom. The lip of the wave pitches forward and often forms a tube. Take-offs on reefs can be very difficult because the waves break so quick and hollow – more about this in Chapter 3.1 "Surfing Hollow Waves". The reef itself can be either a rocky, volcano or coral one. The advantage of reef breaks is that it is easy to judge where the waves will start to break due to the never changing shape of the reef (as opposed to ever-changing sandbars). The take off area is usually well defined and it is merely a matter of skill how close (or even beyond) the critical take-off spot is as you paddle for the wave. Around the reef the water

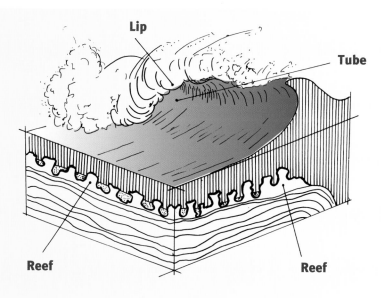

Lip

Tube

Hollow top to bottom wave on reef bottom

Reef

Reef

(Drawing: Stefan "Muli" Müller)

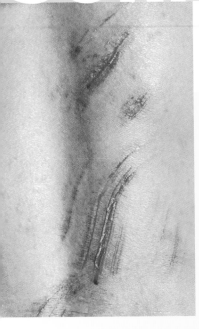

is deeper and sometimes no waves break there at all. The surfer is usually able to paddle around the breaking waves and out the back quite easily.

In places like Fiji or Indonesia this can be rather extreme. The boats that take you out to the reefs sometimes anchor 50 metres away from absolutely huge waves, while the local captain is nonchalantly taking a nap because he knows that he is parked in safe waters.

It is a great feeling to surf in beautifully clear water over coral reef. But everything has its price. Coral reefs are often as sharp as a razor, and infested with sea urchins. Wipe-outs can be quite nasty. Surfing on reefs is only for the expert. So, if you still have difficulties to make the take-off on a hollow beachbreak

Some souvenirs from Indonesia come for free (Photo: "Dr. Surf" Thomas Herold)

wave – leave the reefs alone! Boots and sometimes even a helmet can be necessary. It is worth remembering that coral is a living organism. If you cut yourself, there is always the danger of a painful infection when tiny particles remain in the wound. This is why we usually carry a toothbrush and disinfectant to brush the wound absolutely clean. Wiping the wound with a cut open lime or lemon does the trick as well. A bit painful, but very effective. You will learn to accept the pain of this special treatment after only once having your whole leg, or some other part of the body, swollen and puffy after receiving only a little reef scratch. Surfing on reefs is breathtaking and exciting, but dangerous. Some of the best reef breaks are Pipeline (North Shore, Oahu, Hawaii), Cloudbreak (Fiji), Uluwatu (Bali, Indonesia) and G-Land (Java, Indonesia).

Point Break

On a "point break", it is not only the sea bottom that causes the wave to break. The main characteristic of a point break is a headland (or point) that reaches out into the sea. The wave's energy concentrates itself against the tip of the headland. Here the wave starts to break and runs along the land. Point breaks deliver the longest rides of all. At a point break you can usually take-off in several places. The main and most critical take-off zone is usually at the spot where the wave first meets the headland. This makes the take-off difficult, above all when there are lots of surfers in the water who are all fighting for the inside position in a small take-off area. As you are often surfing along, quite close to a rock-lined headland, a point break can be dangerous. If you wipe-out directly after the take-off it is quite easy to get washed into the rocks. Some of the most well-known point breaks are Jeffrey's Bay (South Africa), Rincon (California) and the legendary Kirra (Australia) which unfortunately has somewhat disappeared for the time being.

The speed and power with which a swell arrives on a beach, reef or point depends on whether the wave breaks on the mainland or on an island. Waves that break on islands such as Hawaii, Fiji or Tahiti are faster and have significantly more power than waves breaking on mainland shores such as France or California. Most of the Pacific islands have volcanic origins. They rise up out of the water steeply, and the waves do not lose speed as they meet the island shores. Waves travelling over underwater continental shelves lose some of their power and speed before they finally reach the mainland shores. There are some exceptions like the waves in Hossegor, France. This is because, in the region of Hossegor, the European continental shelf buckles downward allowing the waves to hit the shore hardly without losing any power on their way.

Well, we have managed to fight our way through this dusty bit of theory – hard work, eh? At least, you now know (almost) all there is to know about weather, wind and waves, and you will really be able to annoy your friends with all your smart comments on your next surfari. OK, once again, repeat after me: an isobar is ... Stooooop! That's enough!!!

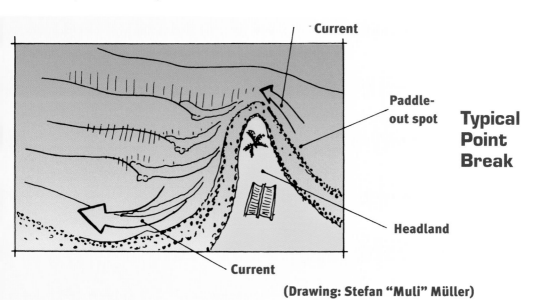

Current

Paddle-out spot

Typical Point Break

Headland

Current

(Drawing: Stefan "Muli" Müller)

Serious Fun!

(Photo: Bill Morris, O'Neill)

3 Let's Get Serious!

What do you mean 'serious'? We just want to have fun. Of course, but part of the fun is the adrenaline rush you get when a big sneaker wave set appears on the horizon; when you paddle for a sucking top-to-bottom wave; when you pull into a tube or when you can see the razor sharp reef through the water during the take-off. The only really dangerous thing of all these is the reef. Everything else is mainly just buzzing around in your head. By saying 'serious' we obviously do not mean that the fun will stop – quite the contrary. However, demanding waves will need skill, concentration and commitment. The following chapter is therefore for everyone, who generally does not fall during the take-off, can surf backhand almost as well as forehand and who is not afraid of waves in the 2-4 feet range.

3.1 Surfing Hollow Waves

When we talk about a hollow wave we mean a wave that breaks top-to-bottom. The particular thrill of these waves is, on the one hand, the speed at which they break, and thus the speed at which you will ride them. On the other hand, hollow waves allow you to get tubed. This is the case when behind the part of the wave which is breaking downward, a sort of pocket or tunnel is formed. A good surfer can ride, depending on the wave, in this tunnel for a few seconds (which will appear like ages once you are in there). You cannot see the surfer from the beach anymore. He is actually inside the wave until he hopefully comes flying out again at the end. This manoeuvre rates very high in competitions, and most surfers would agree that getting 'tubed', and to emerge at the end of it, is easily the best feeling in surfing. But to get this far there a few things that you will have to master first.

The most critical moment on a hollow wave is the take-off. You will only have a fraction of a second to stand up and get into position on your board. This means that your movements and actions must be perfected and automated. The first few times that you are confronted with a really hollow wave your heart will probably sink into your boots and you will instinctively pull back. You paddle for the wave, and at the moment that you want to stand up the wave is already so steep that you can hardly see the face of it, and you are looking directly down at the bottom of the wave. If you have ever dropped into a halfpipe on a skateboard with a good "vertical", you will know the feeling. It actually feels as if there is no way you are going to make it. However, you will be surprised – there is. In addition paddling is often more difficult because of all the water being sucked up by the face of the hollow wave from the bottom. Waves like this are called "sucky waves". This makes it very hard to catch the wave at just the right moment. But getting in early is essential if you want to make the drop. To catch the wave in spite of all this there is only one recipe – paddle hard! The speed of your paddling is crucial. The faster you are, the better. Note the following rule – a hollow wave breaks fast so you must paddle fast to catch it; simple. The steepness of the wave may tempt you to think that it will be easy to catch. Wrong!

It often also helps to paddle additionally with your feet to gain some extra speed in the critical phase before you stand up. In any case, do not forget the two extra arm strokes. Also in hollow waves it sometimes helps to move your centre of balance forward by lying a little forward on the board. The wave is so steep that, when paddling, the nose is lifted out of the water anyway so it does not dig in so easily. The forward leaning position gives you more downward pressure to overcome the upward sucking motion of the wave. It is worthwhile experimenting a little with your position on the board. Lying further forward also helps if, in addition, an offshore wind is blowing against you. The board sits deeper in the water and gives less resistance to the wind.

A further trick in steep, sucky waves and a strong offshore wind, despite everything we told you, is to relax the overstretched back position and press the chest down onto the board. This way you are slightly pushing the board down the wave. Just try it – it works.

A further important factor are the thoughts that are going through your head. Up to now you have probably often paddled for a wave, looked down it and then pulled back because you thought it was too steep for you. These times are over. Decide beforehand whether you are going to take the wave or not. If it is too big or too steep – OK leave it and let it pass through. If, however, you decide to go for

Pretty steep

(Photo: Bill Morris, O'Neill)

a wave, you must give it all you have got to actually catch it. Never hesitate while you are paddling for a hollow wave. This will mainly lead to you slowing down and getting stuck in the lip and freefalling down the wave – wipe-out! Instead, paddle and stand up as fast as possible. This is all you should ever think about during the take-off. So, if you paddle for a wave, the decision must have been made whether you are going to take-off on this one or not.

Now to the drop itself. The important thing is not to surf straight down the wave face with the surfboard lying flat on the surface. Because the wave breaks in a concave form, there is a sharp bend at the bottom of it. The surfboard cannot manage this bend if it sits flat on the surface. The nose digs into the water and someone else rides your tube.

The trick is to surf down the wave at a sideways angle. This way the bottom of your surfboard does not lie flat on the surface but the inside rail holds your surfboard in the wave. The sooner you can press this inside rail into the wave face the better. Therefore, surf down the wave diagonally from the take-off. Just imagine you are traversing down a steep hill on a snowboard and are riding only on the edge of the board. Thin surfboards have a big advantage here. Logically a thin rail cuts through deeper than a thicker one. The board sits deeper in the water and has more stability. If you are riding on the rail the board will be able to ride much easier over the bend at the base of the wave. The curve or rocker of your board matches the bend of the wave. It is essential to apply enough pressure to the inside rail; respectively on the balls of your feet, if you are surfing frontside, and on your heels when you are surfing backside. Some people find it even easier to make the drop backside because they are able to put more pressure on the inside rail by using their heels. Hollow waves often lead to spectacular wipe-outs. Despite all this great advice, you will be late standing up, getting stuck in the lip and come unavoidably crashing down the wave. This is all part of it. Make sure that as you fall, you push your board away from you somehow. Water is soft – your board is not. After several freefalls you will soon know how to safely get to the bottom of the wave. Once you are relatively confident in hollow waves (if you can ever really be so), you will find they are what one metre of fresh powder snow is for the snowboarder– the cream on the cake.

When you surf in hollow waves, sooner or later, whether intentionally or unintentionally, you will find yourself in a tube – but then what?

Tube Riding

Whether you want to or not, sometime or other you will get into the tube – the barrel – the green room, or whatever you want to call it. If the waves are breaking hollow enough getting into the tube is not a problem. The difficult part is being able to stay on your board and getting out of the tube again. While many cool Hawaiians just give a short nonchalant nod after riding a 5-metre wave, they yell an excited "yeah" after being spat out at the end of big barrel. Where swells come rolling in through deep waters and suddenly hit a shallow reef the waves do not simply roll out. Instead the lip pitches forward in a big arch. Behind the lip is the pocket, which all surfers seek. If the wave starts to break in relatively deep water, which provides an easy entry and take-off, it is not hard to get into the tube when the wave then hits a shallower part of the reef further down the line and throws out. You are already up and riding in a safe stance as the lip pitches. You ride as closely as possible to the wall of the wave, avoiding being thrown off as the lip flies over you. Flex your knees and bend down to make yourself as small as possible on the board. If you look around now you will find yourself enclosed by the wave for a short moment. You are in the tube. It will then probably just go bang and you will again do the full washing cycle as the wave breaks all over you when the tube shuts down. Never mind – let's try again. What we have described above, getting into the tube so easily and almost automatically is, however, rare. You will have to practice how to get into the tube on purpose. There are two ways of doing this. The first way is to actually slow down to let the breaking wave and the tube catch up with you. This is called a "stall". The second way is to take-off so far away from the shoulder, i.e., right on the inside, that you can only make the section of the wave that is breaking down in front of you if you drive through it rather than around it. You will actually surf into the tube from behind it – this is why it is called "to backdoor". The difference between the two techniques is obviously that by stalling you brake to enter the tube, and by backdooring you have to put your foot down and speed up to get barrelled. Once in the tube things pretty much stay the same.

It is important to keep pressure on the inside rail. It holds your surfboard on the vertical part of the wave. According to how far you are inside the tube, you have to increase or decrease your speed by slightly changing your position on the board. A little to the front increases your speed, and a little to the rear slows you down. Next time you see a video of a surfer coming out of the tube, watch where he is standing on the board which is usually way forward. The stall comes easier when you use your arm or your hand as a brake. When surfing forehand it is your rear hand that drags along the wave to slow you down. This also gives you some additional stability. On your first attempts to get tubed, you will often surf in front of the tube without actually being in it. The only thing to help you here is to move your weight onto the rear foot, and stick your hand into the wave face until the lip catches up with you – then, knock the brakes off and put your foot down again. As you improve your tube riding skills you will learn to adjust the timing of your bottom turn to help your positioning for the tube without having to stall too hard for it.

How deep can you go?

(Photo: Tim Jones, Billabong)

The problem with these wonderful tubes is that they often hand out a decent bashing if you do not make it. This often includes getting bounced on the more or less hard or sharp bottom (remember, hollow waves break in shallow water). In spite of all this, practice is the only way to learn. That means taking almost every opportunity to pull into a tube. In small waves this is not such a big deal, but in 6 to 8-footers, with a 2-foot thick lip flying over the top of you, it can be quite intimidating. You will often see a surfer watching his friend surf and yelling at him to, "Pull in"! What this really means is, "Don't dodge the tube or you'll be a loser forever." This is why the surfspot "Pipeline" in Hawaii (one of the biggest and most dangerous tubes around) has been given the nickname "The Banzai-Pipeline" after the Japanese Kamikaze pilots' war cry before killing themselves. In order to avoid some of the wipe-outs, at the moment when the situation just becomes 'unmakeable,' you can turn the nose of your board hard into the wave face in order to try to punch through the back of the wave. Unfortunately this only works sometimes. If you fall off inside the tube, it is important that you somehow get away from your board. The best way to do this is to do a dive forward in the direction you are surfing and towards the possible exit window at the last moment. You can also fall off the back of the board pushing it away with your feet. The wave will still eat you, but you will at least have a greater chance of not hitting your board. One thing to remember, if you jump off, jump in parallel to the wave – and not in the direction of the beach!

Getting tubed on your backhand is a particular challenge. The trick here is to do a so-called "pig-dog". Standing sideways on your board with your back to the wave you will stall by twisting your forward (in relation to the tip of your board) shoulder back, and, using the arm belonging to it, drag your hand in the water. At the same time your rear hand grips the outside rail just somewhere near your forward foot. Now look at yourself and you will know why it is called a 'pig-dog'.

The advantage of this stance is that you can shift your weight back and forth without losing your balance. Grabbing the rail gives you greater stability and rail pressure in steep waves. Additionally it will automatically make you bend down to fit the tube. It is better to practice this movement a few times on the beach so that in the water (or even in the tube) you do not have to think too much about it. The key to making a backhand-tube-ride is really the forward shoulder. So, do yourself a favour and twiiiiist it around. Just to avoid any confusion once again: regulars turn the left shoulder to the rear and grab the rail with the right hand. Goofys do the opposite; turn the right shoulder and grab with the left hand. Only the hottest surfers can ride a tube backside without pig-dogging. This is then called, however, a "no-hands tube".

Finally the most important tip of all: keep your eyes open inside the tube! First of all it looks pretty cool inside the tube anyway, and secondly you must focus on reaching that exit, the light at the end of the tunnel. As long as you can see it there is still a chance that you will make it through. Pull in!

(Photo: Bill Morris, O'Neill) **Pig-dog Tube**

by a regular foot on his backhand

3.2 Surfing Big Waves

Defining "big waves" already poses a major problem. What is big? What is small? Here is an example. When we were in Australia surfing big waves, as far as we were concerned anyway, we felt like excited kids after each of us had caught a few waves, and had arrived back on the beach safe and sound to tell of our heroic efforts on the high seas. We were sure that we had surfed some absolutely gigantic mountains, but our Australian friend Pete only remarked in true Aussie style : "Naah mate, that wasn't even six foot." What, not even six feet! When we were in the water we had the feeling that we were paddling around between floating houses. Well, that is the thing with wave heights. It is all very subjective, and wave heights are described differently from country to country. It is also quite common, all over the world by the way, to understate modestly when someone is watching and to grossly over exaggerate when no one is. The kings of understatement are quite definitely the Hawaiians. They calculate practically one to one − metre for foot. This means that conditions upwards of 8 "Hawaiian" feet are not for the faint-hearted. When a Hawaiian surf report tells you that Sunset beach is breaking at 8 to 10 feet, it will be better for you to take your camera and a hat to the beach and leave your surfboard at home. Guaranteed, the waves will be bigger than anything you have ever surfed or even seen before. There is something like an unwritten guide to wave sizes though, which gives you a little understanding and the ability to judge surf and wave reports anywhere you are (except maybe Hawaii for reasons mentioned). Waves are measured in feet, however it is not really about actually measuring exact wave heights, but more a question of putting waves into a category. "And the nominees are ..."

- Up to 2 feet: not real waves, but always better to go for a paddle than sitting around on the beach.

- Up to 4 feet: small waves, lots of fun.

- 4 feet: ideal fun waves to practice manoeuvres and for a relaxed surfing session.

- 5 feet: more fun than serious, but some adrenaline.

- 6 feet: lots of adrenaline! Do not underestimate them, 6-footers are already quite big and powerful– bring a bigger board if you can.

- 6 to 8 feet: (for whatever reason there is really not such a thing as a 7-footer), the same as 6-foot but watch out for larger sets, ride a semi gun if possible, now and again you will be scared.

- 8 feet: really intense waves – big waves – think carefully whether you should go out. Your heart is already beating fast while you are still on the beach, just wait until you are in the water. Sets will send everybody scratching for the horizon.

- 8 or 10 feet: (once again – no such thing as a nine-footer) If you are a good surfer and do not have any problems with 6-foot waves, put your fear aside, paddle out and try to make it safely but full of adrenaline back to the beach.

- 10 feet: this is really the limit for most average surfers. If conditions are clean, i.e., smooth water surface, well co-ordinated sets, clearly defined line-ups and no waves higher than 10 feet, you can paddle out and have a look around. Decide for yourself whether to take a wave; a large board is imperative. "Do not get caught inside" – which means:

Do not get caught by large sets. This is because the impact zone – where the lip comes crashing down – will be really serious and dangerous. It is no crime if you make your way back towards the beach without having caught a wave!

Without wanting to dramatize things here we could actually stop here, because to be true, for most of us mere humans there are very few opportunities of ever surfing anything bigger than 10-foot successfully. Never mind! 10-foot waves are quite sufficient to be able to tell a story or two to your grandchildren sometime or other – even more so as the waves in your story tend to grow in size over the years anyway.

**Check out the photographer
in the upper right hand corner**

**At 10 foot plus even taking pictures becomes a challenge
(Rider: Andy Irons, Spot: Teahupoo, Photo: Tom Servais, Billabong)**

10 foot and over can really be life-threatening depending on how the waves break and on which bottom – so no misjudged heroics! The adrenaline factor will be multiplied several times if the waves are breaking top-to-bottom. If waves break on a shallow reef things will already get quite interesting from 4 feet upwards also.

From around 18 feet plus, an entirely different world begins. Only the top surfers in this world successfully ride those 20-foot mountains. This is a surfing league on its own. Also, there are very few surfing spots in the world that hold this sort of waves where you can surf waves of that size at all. Even in Hawaii there are perhaps only three to four surfspots, which can handle this size. The best known big wave spots around the world are: Waimea Bay and Jaws (Hawaii), Todos Santos (Mexico) and Mavericks (California). Have a look at theses waves on film or in real life from the beach. However, it should not be your aim in surfing to have a go at them. This would be rather frustrating unless of course you live near those waves and start early.

Another popular way to describe waves is to compare them to the size of an average man who is about 1,80 m tall and riding on a wave.

Waves are the described with the relation of the crest or lip of a wave to a surfer riding at the bottom of the wave in full upright position. They categories are rather self explanatorily described as :

- Waist or hip high (2 ft)
- Chest high (2-4 ft)
- Head high (4-6ft)
- Overhead (6 ft)
- Double overhead (twice the full size of the surfer) (6-8 ft)
- Triple overhead (8-10 ft)

As mentioned before, 10 feet is really the limit for most so this is why we want to talk about waves between the 5 to 10 feet range in the following sections on big waves. For some, fear will set in a little earlier, and for others a little later. Generally, however, anything above 6 feet deserves some respect.

There are a few things that are vital to enjoy riding big waves:

1. A surfboard around 7 foot long.
2. A strong and longer (than normal) leash.
3. You must be able to duck-dive well – confronted with 5-foot wave breaking in front of you, you do not bail out, instead pull off your absolutely best duck-dive.
4. You need to be in good shape.
5. You feel at home and have no fear in 4 to 5-foot waves.

Got your board waxed? – Then let's go! But wait a minute – the surf check – more important then ever.

It is extremely important to know whether boomer or clean up sets (larger than the average size on that day) are coming through in regular intervals or not. They are no problem as long as you recognise them early enough as they appear on the horizon so you can paddle over them (or even catch them). This will however only be possible if you maintain a constant lookout for the big sets. When you spot them you must know which way to paddle to get out of their way. Depending on where you are surfing it can be better not to head straight out, but additionally to cut across diagonally towards a possible deep water channel that is hopefully still there.

Before picking a wave it is important to know whether you can ride it all the way, or whether you will have to exit early over the back of it in order to avoid a long and exhausting paddle back out. In big waves it is no surprise that after the euphoria of making the drop, or perhaps getting a tube, you will want to surf for as long as possible. This however is only advisable if the wave ends in or near a deep water channel that allows you to easily paddle back out again without having to do a zillion duck-dives.

This brings us to another point. An important psychological factor is how easy or how difficult you find it to get out to the line-up. Despite excellent duck-diving techniques, it can be frustrating and intimidating when you have to battle for ages to get out at all. Thus, a good knowledge of the local conditions is essential. You need to be able to take advantage of currents to make your way out the back

"Big Waves"
sometimes as thick as they are high

Hawaiian power (Photo: Erik Aeder, Chiemsee)

easier and save energy. Let's have a look at a typical big-wave-day on a beach break. Some way out to sea the waves are breaking on a sandbank. The white water rolls all the way to the beach. If, during your surf check, you spot an area near the outside sandbank without white water pushing through and where hardly any waves are breaking – a sort of passage – then of course you know where you want to paddle out. Sounds simple, but the problem is that you have to do about 20 duck-dives through the white water in order to even reach this passage. With a current running sideways at the same time, you lose a few metres every time you duck-dive. If you try paddling directly towards the passage it is more than likely that you will never reach it because you will be driven off-course by the current. Therefore take the current into account and enter the water 100 or so metres upstream so to say and gradually make you way towards the passage. Getting out through the white water is a problem that does often not exist at reef and point breaks. The waves break only in a well defined area. Away from the reef the water is deeper and hardly any waves break here. In addition there is often a current running between reefs which makes the paddling out even easier. At point breaks, where waves only break along a headland, occasionally you can simply enter the water on the other, protected side of the headland. This way you actually paddle into the line-up from behind. Another – somewhat risky – possibility is to jump off the rocks at the tip of the headland and with a few strokes you find your-self directly behind the breakline. Doing this gets you out into big waves, almost with your hair still dry so to speak. Obviously, timing the incoming waves right is critical as it is too easy to get washed off the rocks while you stand and wait for the right moment to jump. On one hand this way of getting out is simple and saves energy. On the other, for the inexperienced surfer or beginner, the natural barrier of the white water, mentioned earlier, is no longer there so with little effort he has launched himself into conditions that may be too big for his degree of skill.

Currents around reefs and entering the water by jumping off the rocks bear another danger. The entry and exit points in and out of the water are often in different places. This means that beforehand you should take a good look at where and how other surfers are exiting the water. Often beaches are dotted with outcrops of rocks and reefs, and there are only a few spots where you can come in unharmed. This is particularly critical in big waves. For example, in Uluwatu (Bali, Indonesia) the entry and exit point is through a cave. Paddling out of the cave is

Big Waves

simply more time to ride

(Scott Needham, Billabong, snp5000.com)

not a problem, but with big waves and a strong current, finding your way back into the cave demands a certain amount of skill and courage. So, first of all watch and learn from the others.

Currents in big waves can be extremely strong. One spot we surfed in Tahiti, where 4 to 5-footers were good fun, turned out to be totally different and intimidating at 6 to 8-foot. There was so much water moving between the reef that you had to keep paddling very hard just not to get sucked out to sea. Of course, this was very tiring and we soon decided we had had enough. If the current is running towards a harbour wall, rocks, dry reef or something similar it can get dangerous. You must leave the water before you get too exhausted. If you do not feel 100% – maybe a hangover from the night before – you should be realistic about what to expect in the water and what you will be capable of.

Now let's get down to actually surfing big waves. Believe it or not it is almost simpler than surfing small waves. The reason being you have just a little more time for everything. Above all, this is because there is simply more wave to surf on. You can really get the feeling of gliding. The drop lasts longer; the same applies for the bottom turn or the cutback. A larger surfboard will allow you to catch the wave early. You can possibly correct your stance and keep on riding in a firm position. A low stance with bent knees is important to be able to absorb possible chops on the surface of the wave which tend to become more of an issue the bigger the waves get.

When you are surfing your movements should be smoother and with more flow compared to surfing small waves. Look at it this way: when you are driving at top speed on the freeway you really do not want to be making any radical movements with the steering wheel. Big waves therefore are somewhat the freeway of surfing (sounds cheesy, we know).

Top turns are no longer done right on the lip or top of the wave, and generally the manoeuvres become a little less radical. The waves are what makes surfing big waves radical. Otherwise, you do everything else as usual. There is really not much else to tell you on the technique itself. This said your capability to ride big waves depends largely on what is going on in your head. A little bit of angst and adrenaline is OK, but you should never panic because this will eventually lead to dangerous mistakes. This starts with the take-off. At all costs do not hesitate. In big waves the worst type of wipe-out happens when you hesitate and then go over the falls and come crashing with the lip of the wave. If your drop is successful for the first half and you "only" wipe-out at the base of the wave it is not even half as bad. So, just like in hollow waves, when you have decided to go for a wave, give everything to really catch it. Also, here it is important to give the two extra strokes even if you think you have caught the wave. Try to remain relaxed in the water even if the waves are awesome. You can work on this as you continually expand your ability and limitations. If you are still a little afraid in 5-foot waves, you should soon think about having a go at your first session in 6 to 8-footers. Put yourself in the state of mind that you do not necessarily have to take a wave and that you are just there to learn. Keep yourself near one of the channels and watch out particularly for big sets. Just getting used to and dealing with these kind of conditions will make your next session back in 5-footers that much easier. Best of all make your first attempts in big waves in the company of people who are more experienced or better surfers than you are. They can give you advice on where to sit and wait for waves and above all they will make the whole atmosphere a bit more relaxed. If nevertheless you are caught by surprise by a boomer set and a huge foam wall is coming at you, your instinct demands that you throw away your board and dive underneath the wave. In big waves this can be disastrous. If you do not duck-dive properly, and the wave is powerful enough, it will rip your leash off as if it were nothing. The result is that you will be drifting around in huge surf without your surfboard. On top of this a powerful wave may even break your beloved board in half like a matchstick. Apart from the danger that your loose board (still attached to your foot or not) will present to all the others in the water, you should think carefully about whether you want to go through all of this if you decide to bail out and not duck-dive. Even if you are thrown around and bashed about, you will still have your surfboard after a duck-dive, and in big waves this can be vital. There are, however, situations when a duck-dive is impossible. This happens mostly when the wave breaks immediately in front of or over you. All you can do is to get off the board, and, before the wave hits you, give the board a push so that it moves away parallel to the wave e.g., parallel to the beach. This reduces the risk of breaking it, since logically it is easier to break a matchstick (your surfboard) sideways rather than lengthways. But again, you should bail out in an emergency only.

Now for a few important "psycho tips" that will perhaps sound a bit stupid, but which can really be quite effective. We are sure that after a while you will of course develop your own arsenal of motivation tricks.

- Before going into the water say to yourself, "Unreal-big waves at last!" and not "Oh my god, they are huge!"
- If the wave holds you underwater, just think of yourself as a cork in the water. You will come back up again. Don't fight the turbulence when it is strongest to avoid losing too much oxygen too early. Keeping your eyes open and counting helps you avoid panicking.
- Fire yourself up with other surfers to go for the waves. Just as you are about to hesitate on the take-off a loud "Go, go, goooo!" from your buddies works wonders.

Before you go surfing, listen to the music that motivates you the most. There is nothing worse than having a poor song drumming in your mind during big wave sessions. We find that hard and fast music does the trick best for us in big conditions. But each to his own. Who says you cannot pull into a perfect 6 foot tube after a bit of Beethoven.

3.3 Manoeuvres for the Advanced

Actually, we have already described the most important manoeuvre – the tube. But you are right, if you spend all your time in the tube, you will never get a real surfie sun tan. So here are a few more tips for additional radical manoeuvres.

We could draw endless sketches on when and where you have to turn your shoulder, or at what angle you have to stretch your arm out in any particular manoeuvre. Our view is that you will find this out for yourself after a while. But, there are a few things that, if you keep them in the back of your head when you are surfing the next time, will be quite useful.

as radical as can be

"Snap!"

(Photo: Bill Morris, O'Neill)

Off-the-lip

The off-the-lip turn is a great manoeuvre to learn. Simply because you will find it good fun from the beginning and you will be able to do it even more radically as your skills improve. It is not difficult to learn. In its various different versions you will hear an off-the-lip also being called "re-entry" (or 'reo') and "off-the-top" amongst others. It is all about one thing: doing a top-turn, not only when you are at the top of the wave, but right where the lip begins to break and then doing a turn on or with the lip and through this building up more speed. The difficulty is that the very thing on top of which you want to turn, is coming towards you. Once again it is a question of timing. If you are too far away from the curl, the turn will be, firstly very difficult, and secondly, there will be no lip there for your off-the-lip turn. This means that you really have to do the turn where the wave begins to break. The key to a successful off-the-lip is the angle at which you approach the lip.

The more vertical you approach the lip, the easier the actual turning movement, but the more radical the manoeuvre will be. Vertical means that you will practically be going straight up the wave face. The aim is that the lip hits the bottom of the board, and not the side or your feet. After your bottom turn, you are not heading towards the safety of the shoulder, but vertically upwards to the lip. The later you meet the lip as it comes down, the more vertical your board will lie

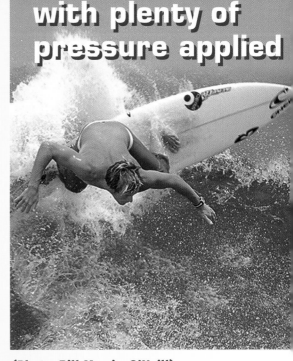

"Backside off the lip" with plenty of pressure applied

(Photo: Bill Morris, O'Neill)

on the wave at the moment of the turn. If you do not have sufficient power in your legs or your timing is wrong, it is possible that the lip will knock your board straight into your face. Be careful! The moment that you turn on the lip is almost like hitting it, hence the expression "to hit the lip". Well, you know, sometimes it seems the lip can also hit back.

Floater

This manoeuvre has actually not been around for that long. We can still remember when we were in France checking the surf in Anglet (near Biarritz) and one surfer in the water was surfing better than anything we had seen there before. He was not only faster and caught the waves further outside than the rest of the people in the water, he somehow simply rode over the white water when a wave closed down in front of him and continued his ride on the unbroken part of the wave – just like that. "Hey this guy just did an ... um ... err ... what-shall-we-call-it ... a floater!" It turned out that the surfer was Tom Curren who was the dominating surfer in the eighties, and still today is seen as one of the best surfers of all times.

The idea of floater is to get over and past a section of the wave that is breaking down in front of you, and continue to ride the open face of the wave beyond it. Before someone had invented the floater (it was not Tom Curren), once a section broke in front of you the ride was pretty much over. So, the floater is a very practical manoeuvre. Again the deciding factor (for any radical manoeuvre for that matter) is speed, vitesse, tempo. If you do not have enough of it the floater will not work. So you build up your speed by trimming up and down the face, because you realise that the section in front of you is about to close down. At the moment the wave breaks, you ride onto and over the foam. You are now actually going against the energy of the wave. If you do not have enough speed the wave will simply throw you off the board. But, how do you get onto the foam? At the moment you reach the white water you have to unweight your board. Just imagine as if you had foot straps on your board and you wanted to jump up with your board. Now adjust the motion to the fact that you actually do not have foot straps. Of course you do not want to jump right up otherwise your board will logically be left behind.

(Photos: Kelly Smith, Smico/Surfer: Beau Atchison)

"Floater..."

Nevertheless, you have to really take the weight off both of your feet. The foam underneath will press the board up and ensure that you do not lose it. Additionally you can somewhat raise your arms to assist the unweighting action. Once again you should make sure that the bottom of the board rather then the nose or rail hits the breaking part of the wave. Try to lift the nose of your board up just before you meet the foam so that the wave only comes into contact with the underside of the board and glides along it.

By the way, river surfing also works on this principle. You are not flushed away by the stream of the river because it is passing underneath the bottom of the board – endless floater so to speak.

The difficulty with the floater is that, firstly, going against the flow of the wave slows you down, which makes keeping your balance difficult, and secondly it is not easy to control your board because the fins have no grip in the foam.

The landing is also not as simple as it seems. Often the transition from the foam to the unbroken part of the wave is somewhat rough. You must keep your knees bent and absorb the impact of the transition as you leave the foam. It is possible that you will actually do a little free fall before you connect with the unbroken part of the wave. Did we say free fall? It seems this is a good point to move on to the next section.

Aerial

Aerials originally where introduced through skateboarding. Skateboarders are able to jump out of a half-pipe and land back down in it again. All this without foot straps. This meant they had to develop a technique of grabbing the board with one or two hands in mid air to make sure the board stayed connected to their feet while they went flying over the rail or coping of the half-pipe. Since many skateboarders are also surfers, it was only a question of time before the first surfers would be jumping out over the top of the waves and landing back on them again. One of the first to do aerials successfully was the South African Martin Potter. In the meantime however an aerial with a built-in 180° or 360° spin belongs to the standard repertoire of each serious new schooler. Aerials are great fun and look spectacular but actually have no real

Get Air!

(Photo: Kelly Smith. Smico, Surfer: Matt Wilkinson)

purpose (like for instance the floater has). But since most useless things often provide the best fun, here are a few tips. Practice your first aerials like a skate-board "ollie hop". This means jumping as you go along by doing a sort of flicking movement with your feet (there's really no other way to describe it), thereby lifting your board up at the same time. The flicking movement is done by pushing down your rear and your front foot quickly one after the other starting with the rear. You can use little chops on the wave as launch pads to make things easier.

The other way of doing an aerial is to start doing an off-the-lip without actually turning on impact with the lip. Instead, you just shoot off over the lip. Once again speed is the key for success. Being able to land after an aerial is usually more by accident than design, but there are many hot rippers out there who regularly pull them off even in contest situations. It is particularly critical that you do not lose contact with the board while you are in the air. If your board lands just ahead of you and you then try to land on your board it will surely be the end of your trusted fibreglass friend. This is why you need to grab the board while in the air with one or two hands just like Tony Hawk or any of the other hot skateboarders. If you want to learn more about how to do various types of aerials we recommend Taj Burrow's"Book of hot surfing". From method airs to superman airs he has got it all wired. Even if you never manage to successfully complete an aerial, just trying is fun enough. So – get air!

The Roundhouse Cutback

Y ou already know about the basic cutback from the section for beginners. If you want to give it a little extra radicalness, first of all put more pressure on the inside rail and lean further into the turn, secondly, drive your board through a full figure eight. Do a cutback in the direction of the breaking wave – and now comes the icing on the cake – you surf back to the breaking lip (actually going against the breaking direction of the wave) and on the oncoming lip you do – yes, just what you thought – an off-the-lip or re-entry, only this time it is called a "rebound". Try to think of it like this: first the cutback then an off-the-lip on the approaching wave. If you can get this into one flowing sequence it looks very fluid and radical.

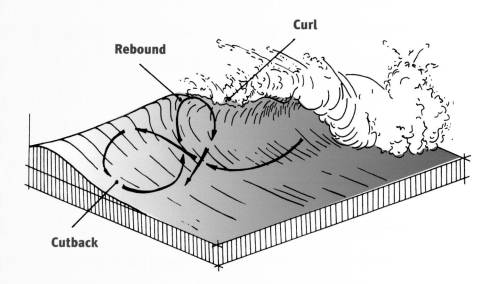

1 x 8 = "Roundhouse cutback"

(Drawing: Stefan "Muli" Müller)

The Snap and/or Tail-slide

A "snap" or "tail-slide" is done almost out on the shoulder (just under or on the edge of the lip). The difference to a normal top-turn is that this manoeuvre is a much more radical and powerful change of direction. You really have to apply a lot of pressure with your rear leg and foot during the turn which then often creates a fountain of water or spray high up over the edge of the wave. This is also called "to throw some spray". The key is the amount of power placed on the rear leg. Just have a look at the legs of Tom Carroll (another 80s legend) and you will know why he is one of the few who pulled off a snap under the lip of a 10 to 12-foot wave at Pipeline, Hawaii. Because of the high pressure on the tail of the board, this will easily break away in a snap, and then you are doing a tail-slide. To be able to control this slide is difficult and requires a lot of body control and flexibility. It is especially easy to do a tail-slide if you do the snap high enough on the wave so that the fins break free beyond the curl, and are practically, for a short time, free in the air letting the board slide over the lip. Here you

(Photo: Kelly Smith, Smico. Surfer: Jono Shade)

Tail Slide

need extraordinary balance not to fall off. The further up the wave you do the snap, the easier it is to push your board through the turn but the harder it is to maintain control. If you do not want to be all that radical, you can do the tail-slide on the shoulder of the wave by pushing the tail round hard and at the same time putting some weight on your front foot. This way the tail lifts slightly out of the water, the fins have less grip, and the turning movement will be easier – allowing you to show off with a funky little tail slide.

Tail-slides, same as aerials, are a bit of a controversial manoeuvre. Some surfers are of the view that they are useless gimmicks compared to a turn where you fully bury your rail. Although, full power turns, from rail to rail, are what performance surfing is all about, tail-slides and airs are great fun and there is no reason why you should not try one. To be able to have the best of both worlds is probably the ideal way, and this is one of the reasons why 8 times world champion Kelly Slater is the dominating surfer of this decade.

The 360°-turn

O f course what we are talking about here is turning through 360° i.e., all the way round in one movement. This is actually a trick, which has regained popularity among the new surfing generation (also called "The New School").

First of all you start a forehand turn up the wave. The tip of your board goes (just like the off-the-lip) straight up the wave only this time you go even further than straight. This means that the tip of the board will drive towards 11 o'clock for goofys and 1 o'clock for regulars (both frontside), with the curl being at 12 o'clock. The lip or the foam presses against the rail now closest to the lip and this pushes you round the roughly remaining 170° of the turn. The critical thing is to go up the wave face "a little more than straight". The remainder is done by the wave almost on its own. Some really hot surfers use the moment when the tail is pointing down to the bottom of the wave to put some weight on to the front foot – the nose – so that they manage to surf backwards for a short time. In the "Surfers Dictionary" you will find this under "reverse". A full carving 360° turn is however a totally different manoeuvre to the little 360° twist we described above and really one of the trickiest moves of the trade that is only ever mastered by a select few including guys like Kelly Slater and Joel Parkinson.

3.4 General Tips for the Advanced

- Reefs are only for the advanced surfer. Although points and sandbanks surely also offer some challenging waves, they usually provide a good ride for everyone.

- Paddle hard in big or hollow waves. Always put in a couple of extra strokes, even when you think you have caught the wave.

- Do not hesitate in large or hollow waves.

- Do not panic underwater. This uses up important energy.

- Learn to control your fears. Develop your own bag of psycho tricks.

- In big waves do not take the first wave of a set. If you then end up not catching it, all the following waves will break on your head.

- Take a good long look at the surfing spot: currents, rocks, shallows, channels, the take-off area, boomer-sets etc.

- Do not panic if your leash breaks. Never try to swim against the current. Always swim back in with the white water and not through the channel.

- Use lulls (pauses between sets) to get out to the line-up.

- Always duck-dive, never bail out.

- The secret for all manoeuvres is speed.

- Getting tubed is the ultimate thrill. Learn to let the tube catch up with you. Keep your eyes open in the tube.

- Get out of the water while you still have enough strength left in you.

- Obey the unwriten rules of surfing. The surfer on the inside always has the right of way.

- "Do not drop-in!" and "Respect the locals!"

- **The most important tip however is: "Get out there and have fun!"**

TIPS

IV WAVES AROUND THE WORLD

Sooner or later a surfer must head out and search for the perfect wave. Even if you have a surfspot right on your doorstep, you will one-day travel to another country to surf unknown waves. Believe us – there are spots out there, where on certain days, things simply come together and the waves can only be described in one word – perfect. To find these places, above all you need two things, time and money. But since time is money, you have solved half the problem already.

Of course, we cannot help you to find the necessary small change for your surfing trip. However, we can help you with saving time on the spot. Where is the surf? How do I get there, and when is the best season? We have gathered quite a bit of useful information from our own travels over the years but it may be worthwhile to get a specific surf travel guide book (e.g. Stormrider guides) for the region you are planning to go to in order to get the complete picture.

Of course, we have not tried every surfspot in the world. We have therefore decided to focus on those places where we have surfed ourselves. If you are interested to hear about where, when and how, join us on this little surftrip around the world.

1 Tips for a Surfari

Where to Go

The factors time and money are the two variables that decide where to go. Surfers are well-known for doing without luxury resorts in exchange for good surf. Who wants a hotel with a pool when 6-foot barrels are breaking on the doorstep? Who wants a breakfast buffet when there is fresh fruit on every street corner? Naturally no-one is against a bit of comfort, but you should really think twice whether you want to invest in an upmarket hotel or in extra miles on

Worth the journey!

(Photo: Menges & Diel)

your air ticket. Our experience is that getting there is usually the most expensive part of the trip. Eating and drinking at home also costs something. If you can manage to keep your expenses for accommodation and travel on the ground (hire car etc.,) to a minimum, you can last for a relatively long time with little money. The secret is to find cheap flights, cheap accommodation and cheap transport.

Time is the other factor that will limit your moves. The shorter the time available, the less time you will want to spend sitting in a car or plane to get there and back. For a one-week trip, a 3-hour flight is more suitable than a 20-hour flight to somewhere like Australia. On top of that there is also the jet lag. Many first time Australia-travellers need a full week to get over the jet lag. It was quite funny when, on our trip through the South Pacific we crossed the International Date Line. We took off on the 9th of June and landed on the 8th of June. We gained a day.

If you have a lot of time, however, it is worthwhile to go looking for 'lonely' waves in exotic places. If time is short, preferably stick to the beaten track where you do not have to go searching for waves and where you know how to read the conditions. A further alternative is to book into a surf camp where, besides transport and accommodation, local knowledge of the area is all-inclusive and provided by the organisers. Surf camps can be found in various places; in Europe, Australia, California and also Indonesia and the South Pacific but more about this later.

Besides having enough time, the wave season in the chosen surfing destination is also a factor. Somewhere in the world there is always someone surfing at any one time. The film, "The Endless Summer", illustrates this in a way that has sent thousands of surfers around the world in search for waves. A frustrating image, however, when you are sitting at home saving for your next surfing trip. In the Northern hemisphere the summer lasts from June to September. In the Southern hemisphere it is exactly the opposite. When it is summer in the Northern hemisphere, it is winter in the southern part, and when the north is shivering in winter (November to February), the south is basking in summer sunshine. But there are places, like Hawaii for instance, where it never gets really cold and the water is always warm, and you can surf all year round (on different coasts though). In several countries there are not four seasons but only the difference between the wet and the dry season. But you should be able to get this sort of information from your travel agent. What he will most likely not be able to answer, is when the waves will be breaking in the different places. The following table will give you a few clues as to where the tubes are hiding at different times of year (the details are based on the Northern hemisphere seasons).

Where to go?	When to go?	Whats cookin
Indonesia		
Bali	March – September	4-10 foot
G-Land	March – September	4-12 foot
Nias/Mentawai	March – September	4-8 foot
Europe		
France	Mid August – October	2-8 foot
Spain	Mid August – October	2-8 foot
Canaries	October – March	2-8 foot
Portugal	October – December	2-8 foot
Australia		
Queensland	January – April	4-8 foot
New South Wales	February – April	2-8 foot
Victoria	March – Oktober	4-10 foot
USA		
California	September – November	4-6 foot
Hawaii	October – March	6-30 foot
South Pacific		
Fiji/Tahiti	April – October	4-12 foot
South Africa		
West Coast	April – October	4-8 foot
East Coast	April – October	2-8 foot
Mexico		
Mainland	April – May/October – September	4-12 foot
Baja	April – Oktober	4-8 foot
Costa Rica	Januar – April	3-6 foot
Indian Ocean		
Réunion	May – September	4-8 foot
Maledives	March – April/September – October	3-6 foot

Spa or Ice cube?	Dress code?
27° C	No suit
27° C	No suit
27° C	No suit
18° C	Springsuit to Fullsuit 3/2
19° C	Springsuit to Fullsuit 3/2
20° C	Springsuit to Fullsuit 3/2
17° C	Streamer 3/2
25° C	No suit to springsuit
20° C	Springsuit/Tubesuit
15° C	Streamer 3/2
19° C	Streamer 3/2
25° C	No suit to springsuit
25° C	No suit
14° C	Fullsuit 4/3
20° C	Springsuit to Fullsuit 3/2
28° C	No suit
20° C	No suit to Fullsuit 3/2
27° C	No Suit
25° C	No suit to tubesuit
28° C	No Suit

If you have made your selection, there are a number of ways to learn more about the land of your dreams. Here are a few for you to choose from:

Have a look on the internet. There are a numerous surf pages with detailed information about different surfing destinations. There are some specialised surfing travel agencies around and you can find out about them in surf magazines or on the Internet. Worldsurfaris and Surf Travel Company (STC) in Australia or Wavehunters in the USA are just a few examples (check the info chapter at the end for the web pages). Their web pages are excellent sources of information on most surf-spots around the world.

You can, however, also invest a little more time and read this book to the end.

What to bring

Packing for a trip. What a great feeling. We assume that you will know for yourself what clothes to take with you – if not just ask your mom. But what surfing equipment do you need? As a basic principle – as much as necessary and as little as possible. Once you have dragged your giant travel bag, plus several surfboards in an even more gigantic board bag, through a steaming hot exotic airport, you will no doubt swear to pack only a fraction next time.

Boards

We always try to take at least two boards with us on our trips. A shortboard about 6.5 feet long for waves up to 5 feet, and a semi gun about 7 feet long for the larger waves. We also really recommend boards with removable fins for travelling. Make sure to check the extra charge the airline will make for carrying your boards. Some will take your stick for free, others will charge so much that you could buy a new board at your destination for the same money.

If you want to, or are only able to take one board with you, it should be an all-round board that should rather be a little longer than normal. You will, of course, need a little more power to push the board around in small waves, which you will soon get used to, but when the waves are solid you will be much more confident and better equipped. You do not have to hold back when you finally find the perfect 6-foot waves you have travelled for.

Board bag

You should always look after and protect your beloved surfboard. Surfboards get easily damaged. On top of this, airport personnel usually do not handle your luggage with the greatest care. In some languages it seems that the sticker "Fragile" means something along the lines of: "This surfboard is especially suitable for throwing the heaviest and hardest piece of luggage on top of it." This is why a board bag is an absolute must. Ideal is a bag that will take at least two boards. If the airline accepts a second piece of luggage without charging extra, you can pass off your second board in one stroke with your double board bag. The board bag should be one with robust exterior material and a reliable solid zip, which you can unzip hundreds of times, despite all the sand and salt-water getting in the works. A board bag may also come in handy as a sleeping bag or mattress for nights under the stars in the open.

Sunblock

If you do not necessarily have to prove that you have had a fantastic trip by showing off a suntan, wearing a wetshirt when in the water is better for your skin. Whether there is a hole in the ozone layer or not, too much sun is bad for your skin. A strong, water resistant suncream and a zinc sun blocker for lips and nose should not be missing from your list.

Wetsuit

When it comes to the wetsuit, you have to know what kind of water temperature to expect at your destination. Even if the water is warm, like for instance in Bali, wearing a vest or something similar can protect you from cuts on a reef. Countries where you should take a wetsuit with long legs and arms are Europe (Spain, France, UK etc.), California, Australia and New Zealand during their winter and autumn and South Africa. In addition take one or two wetshirts for the sun and as protection against getting a rash from the rubbing of your wetsuit. Surf boots are also necessary for all surfing destinations where the waves break over rocks or coral reefs. If you do not intend to be scared of 6-foot top-to-bottom waves, we recommend you also to take a surf helmet.

Other Things

Sooner or later, your surfboard will get a ding. Most little cracks can be repaired by yourself with some resin and catalyst. There are especially made-up repair kits for travelling in which you will find everything you need to do a small repair job. Products such as "Solarez" (resin out of the tube) have proved to be very practical. In this case the resin requires no catalyst, because it is already contained in the product. Ultraviolet rays cause a chemical reaction and the resin hardens in seconds. Make sure to apply the resin in the shade. As soon as the mixture is exposed to sunlight the magic begins to work. The practical part about it is that you will not get the mixing formula wrong and all you have to carry around is a little tube of resin and some sandpaper – just in case anyway.

Travel Guides

Besides a special surfing guide for each country, that will help you to find the best waves, you should also get your hands on a general tourist guidebook with information about currency, health care and services, local customs and habits, accommodation, consulates etc. On our trips the guides from "Lonely Planet" proved to be very useful everywhere we went, especially the tips concerning value for money accommodation and food.

There are many guidebooks around. However, it is not always evident that you will have the same understanding of the words "cheap" or "interesting" as the author of the book.

Health

You should always take a small medical kit with you. Peroxide for disinfecting, medicine against diarrhoea and band aids are all essential contents.

In many exotic countries there is still a threat of malaria (e.g. Mentawais Islands, Indonesia). The danger zones change as rapidly as the most efficient remedies do. An Institute for Tropical Medicine, doctors specialising in tropical medicine, health authorities and some airlines can all give you information regarding the necessary prophylactic measures. However, now close your bag, put the surfboards on the roof rack and let's get moving to the airport. Let's go surfing!

(Photo: Jan "Leo" Leopold)

Always bring
a back-up board
... or two

2 Europe

There is something funny about Europe. All the European surfers want to go to Australia or America, while all the Australians or Americans particularly want to go to Europe to surf. And they are right! In Europe you can find really good waves all year round. The waves are often underrated. The beach breaks in Hossegor, the tubes in Mundaka, the reefs in Portugal and on the Canary Islands are all world-class. There is not much point in trying, in this chapter, to list or describe all the good European spots, because others have already done this in an excellent way. The "Stormrider Guide" by Low Pressure Ltd. describes almost every spot in Europe. It tells you when and where the waves are breaking – if you plan to surf in Europe this guidebook is an absolute 'must-have'. We would like, nevertheless, to tell you about a few of our own experiences to help you on your way.

France

Although we have surfed some good waves on the Mediterranean ocean, we want to restrict ourselves here to the Atlantic coast south of Bordeaux. There are lots of reports and also photos of waves in the Mediterranean – but between you and me, these are only exceptions to the rule. In complete contrast, the Atlantic coast is a totally different story. Of course there are periods, sometimes lasting more than a week, when the Atlantic pretty much resembles the Mediterranean but usually there is always at least a small wave somewhere. You will find waves on the Atlantic coast all year round. However, only the real hard-core surfers go out here in winter because the water is freezing. The best time for waves is late summer to autumn. Since this fact is rather well known round the world, several professional surf contests are held here during this season. That means that from August onwards there is a lot going on in and out of the water at the popular spots, which sometimes creates a bit of an aggressive attitude in the water. The French Atlantic coast, however, has one main disadvantage, which funnily enough turns into an advantage when there are too many people in the water. The disadvantage is that the coast is basically a single, long, straight stretch of beach. This means that when the wind is blowing hard from the north or west, it practically blows out the whole coast, since there are hardly any headlands or bays and only a few rock piers on the whole coast to protect the waves from the wind. As a result, conditions along the coast on any one day are pretty much the same anywhere you go. The big advantage, however, is that if you are at a spot with 50 other people and the surf is pumping, it is very probable that you will find similar conditions on some other beach nearby. Although the conditions are often very similar, there are great differences in the quality of the waves dependent on the sandbanks, on which the waves break. A spot where the waves broke perfectly in one year may produce only close-out waves the next year when the sandbanks have changed. This leads to everybody having his own secret spot on a secret sandbank to go to with a few friends for a quiet session. This is the really fascinating part about France. Although so many surfers go there year after year, you can always find your own secret spot behind Dune No 12.

A further strong influence on the quality of waves is the tide. The differences between low and high tide can be extreme. The waves that break during low tide will often be considerably different to the waves at high tide. Some experience is required to understand all these numerous factors and make use of them. You will soon know when and where the waves are breaking. Two friends, who mastered this many years ago, are Uli and Martin from the surf school "Wave Tours". They are both German, but have been running surf camps in France for many years. They offer fun surf courses for both beginners and the advanced in a relaxed and comfortable camping atmosphere. A course includes accommodation in a top camping site, equipment (including board and wetsuit), transportation to the various surf spots and coaching as well as many other good fun things. The guys from "Wave Tours" have a lot of experience with landlubbers, some of whom we would have written off as absolutely hopeless. Not so Uli and Martin who will never give up until your first wave is successfully ridden. If you want to make your first attempts a lot easier, book a course with Uli and Martin to start with. Advanced surfers can of course also learn a thing or two from them as they are truly seasoned experts. You can check them out on the web at www.wavetours.com. We can recommend the "Wave Tours" boys, not only because of the efficient way they teach, but simply because you will surely have a good time with them and all the other surfers in their camps.

The Atlantic coast is, as we have already said, one single stretch of surfing beach that starts just above Bordeaux and runs down to St Jean de Luz near the Spanish border. Here are some of the best spots.

Lacanau Ocean

The water in summer is still relatively fresh here. In the last few years tourism has rather taken the upper hand in the town itself as far as we are concerned. Accordingly, there is quite a lot of activity in the water. However, to the north and south of the town there are a number of lonely beaches with good waves. In the south, the road (an old tank track) behind the dunes is sometimes closed off. If you park your car, and walk a few metres, you will be able to find a beach almost all to yourself. And for those who do not know yet – you will find out soon enough though – nude sunbathing and swimming is very much the fashion away from the main beaches in France.

Hossegor/ Seignosse

Here you will find some of the most powerful beach breaks on the whole Atlantic coast. Given the right conditions you will have more tubes then you can handle.

The main surf spot in Hossegor actually belongs to the village of Seignosse, and is called les Estagnots. If you are going towards Hossegor, drive in the direction of the sea, and just before you get to the beach go on the road behind the dunes northwards towards Seignosse. As you pass the town signpost the road goes up to the left to Plage des Estagnots or Cote Sauvage (wild coast). You will eventually come to the legendary parking lot, which in the high season, looks more like a campsite with surfers from all over the world. On the beach itself there are three main peaks. Using the lifeguards shed on the dune as 12 o'clock there is usually a wave that breaks directly in a line with this hut. A second wave breaks at 2 o'clock, and a third at 11 o'clock. Surf the one that is least crowded. For whatever reason, surfers tend to suffer from the 'sheep syndrome', because whenever and wherever a couple of surfers are sitting in the water, suddenly the next one paddles out and the next one and so on until the two surfers who where happily enjoying their "quiet" session are eventually merged into a herd of surfers. Do not play this game! In particular if you arrive at a surfspot with a group of friends and there are already other people

Roadtrip

**Life on the legendary Estagnot parking lot
(Photo: Menges/Diel)**

surfing. At least try to avoid behaving like a bunch of sheep. Always check out the uncrowded wave on the next sandbank first. Our view has always been to rather go for the less perfect but also less crowded spots. This said, if you are a beginner it is important to still have someone keeping an eye open for you.

If you follow the signpost to "Front de Mer" in Hossegor you will come to the notorious Rock Food – the favourite surfers hangout with parties, videos etc. When the swell is really big and everything else is closed out, directly in front of Rock Food there is an excellent wave. If you walk some 100m north from there you will find one of the heaviest barrels in the whole of France at La Graviere which only breaks in big swells and is usually the site of the Professional World Tour contest in September if the waves are on. Further to the south of Hossegor, in the town of Capbreton is la Piste, easy to recognise because of the World War II German bunkers that line the beach. This is another quality beach break with numerous peaks to be found north and south of it.

Biarritz

Biarritz is the biggest town on this stretch of coast with plenty of surf shops and many good surf spots. North of Biarritz, in the direction of Bayonne and in a place called Anglet, lies Chambre d'amour. In the shadows of a tall cliff the beach has been artificially divided up into a number of little beaches. Numerous rock piers create particularly interesting sandbank formations with often high quality beach breaks. The locals in Biarritz can sometimes be a little oversensitive so they should be handled with care. Show some respect and you will be fine. North of Chambre d'amour the River Adour flows into the sea. A long stone pier has been built on the south side of the river mouth. Some time ago, one of the best waves in Europe broke on the north side of the pier – La Barre. Today the waves here have lost most of their quality but they are often your last resort if the wind is howling from the south, as the pier offers protection from it. Quality wise it is a different story on the south side of the pier. On the Plage des Cavaliers, the waves are often some of the best in the whole Biarritz area since the stone pier offers good protection from the prevailing northerly winds. Additionally, next to the pier there is a current running out to sea, which you can use like a conveyor belt to get you out into the line-up.

In Biarritz, the main beach itself, la Grand Plage, is relatively well-protected from southerly and northerly winds. However, aggressive and unfriendly locals as well as a high degree of water pollution often spoil the fun here. Our negative highlight in this regard was a dead rat, swollen to easily twice its normal size, that floated past us in the water.

South of Biarritz towards the Spanish border there are actually some reef-breaks, which for France is extremely unusual. These reefs need a strong swell to work properly. Lafitenia has a powerful right-hander, and at Guethary a big perfect A-frame peak breaks left and right. In the town of the same name you drive in the direction of Cenitz or the harbour. The wave breaks about 500m out from the beach. Beyond Guethary keep an eye open for the signpost "Acotz" to get to Lafi-tenia. The road leads up to a large parking place. From here you have to walk down a steep road about 100 m to the beach. The wave breaks to your right. The wave itself can have a challenging somewhat ledgy take-off and offers long and fast rides. Get you hands on a good map and go looking. It is all part of the fun, particularly as there are many more spots and some rather good looking locals in this area which you may well stumble upon.

Spain

North Coast

Coming from Biarritz you drive directly into the legendary Basque country. The Basques are a little reserved when it comes to dealing with tourists and sometimes they can even be somewhat arrogant. However, just as in most places a friendly smile more often than not breaks the ice.

San Sebastian just across the French border has an old part of the town that offers an exciting night-life. The typical Spanish tapas-bars are our favourites. On late weekend nights you could be tempted to think that a big street festival was on, but this is normal night life here. If you take the motorway towards Bilbao you are well on the road to Mundaka and the amazing waves there. At Amorebieta you have to turn off in the direction of Guernica and then towards Bermeo. Just before you get to Bermeo, you land in the town of Mundaka. The waves break in the river mouth directly behind the unmistakable landmark of the village church. Without doubt, Mundaka is the best and longest left wave in Europe and surely it is one of the best in the world. Tubes, tubes, tubes! Although the waves break on a sandy bottom, they are very powerful. Multiple tubes on one single wave are quite common. But you have to be quick. The waves are so long and fast that, after continually pumping, your legs will eventually beg for mercy. Mundaka can be a bit of a Diva as you are never quite sure when she will put on a show. We arrived in Mundaka for the first time at high tide on a smaller swell and immediately thought our journey had been a waste of time because nothing was breaking. As the tide began to go out, the picture changed from one minute to the next, and we could not get into our wetsuits fast enough.

The way out to the line-up goes through the little fishing harbour. You paddle through the absolutely calm waters of the harbour. As soon as you leave the harbour waters, you are off. A strong current running along the harbour wall pulls you straight out into the middle of the line-up. Mundaka has to be handled with caution during a large swell, because the place has a few surprises in store.

The waves break right in the entrance of a river and they depend very much on the tide. When the tide goes out all the water flows out to sea, and in seconds you will be pulled out quite a distance and spend the rest of the time paddling to get back to the line-up. Paddling for the wave, you will also be fighting against the current, resulting in a somewhat late, steep and difficult take-off. As the tide changes this little game runs the other way round. During the incoming tide water is pushed into the river mouth. If you see a big set coming in, and you want to paddle towards it, you will find you are hardly moving because of the current. From 6-foot upward it gets a little hairy. After a successful ride the current in the middle of the rivermouth will make the return to the line-up difficult.

However, you can use the water running out to sea along the harbour wall regardless of high or low tide to get you back to the line-up. When you finish a ride in the middle of the bay you obviously have to paddle a fair distance across and back to the harbour wall and its line-up lift. This same current is also used to get back into the harbour to exit the water. You ride a wave as far as it goes up the river and then paddle across back into the current along the harbour wall, as mentioned already. You must keep a little to the left whilst in the current, and just before the harbour entrance

Mundaka, at full steam, what a sight

Mundacca – what a set up (watch for the current in front of the harbour wall on the very left in the picture) (Photo: Joli)

you have to paddle hard to get out of the current and into the harbour. If you do not keep far enough to the left, you will not make it, and you will have to go full circle again. There is also another exit point into a little bay just below the church which however can be somewhat dangerous in big swells as the bay is lined with big rocks.

The Mundaka locals are a special breed. You could almost call them the matadors of the surf. Whilst no doubt being fearless and relatively aggressive, they sometimes seem to be not fully in control of the waves and themselves. Act friendly and let them have their waves. Arguing is useless. Sometime or other a wave, with your name on it, will come along. So be patient and do not drop in even if local after local eat it after taking off to far inside. If you treat the locals with respect they will leave the odd wave for you. And that is really all you need. A single wave from start to finish in Mundaka is enough freeze a week-long smile on your face.

Around Mundaka, as well as around the region of Zarautz, there are numerous other spots that are worth the trip. So, "Hasta la vista, baby!"

The Canaries

Up until now we have only surfed on the island of Fuerteventura. However, all the islands here offer good surfing. The Canary Islands are the Hawaii of Europe. You will find powerful waves with warm temperatures in the middle of the European winter. The water is not cold, but in winter your wetsuit should at least have long legs and but you may get away with short sleeves.

Fuerteventura
Although waves break practically the whole year, the warm temperatures combined with solid swells in winter are the special attraction. During this time of the year the so-called North Shore comes alive and you will find one quality reef break after the other.

In Fuerteventura your first call should be a chap called Sigi Opitz. He has been living and surfing on Fuerteventura for many years now and knows the place inside out. Together with his girlfriend, Maria, he runs a really cool surf camp in Corralejo called "Ineika Funcenter". Whether you are a beginner in the surf school or an advanced surfer doing a guided tour with Sigi himself, the name Funcenter means exactly that. On top of that, the prices are very reasonable. The vibe at Ineika is easygoing and relaxing. A surf course at Ineika never fails to deliver as having fun is the top priority. You will find people here from all over the world. The quality waves on Fuerteventura do the rest. We have been coming back year after year and have always had a great time and great waves with Ineika, and we are sure you will experience the same.

You can contact Sigi on www.ineika.com. By the way, the airport transfer charge is usually included in the price. Sigi Opitz knows where the Fuerteventura tubes are and believe us he knows how to pull in.

Sigi "Captain Lobos" in his office

(Photo: Sigi Opitz, Ineika Funcenter)

Portugal

The Portuguese Atlantic coast is the ideal spot to get away from the crowds in France. Portugal is pretty far away from any other place in Europe but the often uncrowded quality waves are well worth the extra effort. An alternative is to fly into Lisbon and hire a car there. Some of the surf spots are in the immediate vicinity of the city. Portugal has waves, reasonable prices and the locals are friendly. What else could you be looking for?

The water is super-cold, even in summer. Bring a full suit. Interestingly the temperature of the water in winter does not drop further all that much. Thus, surfing in the colder seasons is still a good option. The best time of year is therefore from September onwards. For your evening entertainment we recommend, besides the local bars, a visit to the local cinema. The movies are in English (with Portuguese sub-titles) and admittance is often dirt cheap.

Although you can surf along the whole of the Atlantic coast as well as parts of the Algarve, the surfing scene is concentrated around the areas of Ericeira and Peniche. Ericeira is well-known for its reefs (infested with sea urchins), which produce fantastic waves. Remember the name "Coxos". On the Baleal peninsula near the town of Peniche you will always find a wave with an offshore wind, irrespective where the wind is coming from because you can surf on both sides of the peninsula. One side has a quality beach break, and the other a good reef with lots of sweet little sea urchins. It is a great area to spend some time. Just around the corner is a famous spot called 'Supertubes' – the name pretty much says it all.

The area around Sagres and Lagos at the southern tip of Portugal also offers some great uncrowded waves. Due to the shape of the coast you are always able to find a spot that is offshore or protected from the wind. Unfortunately this area tends to be a little bit more on the expensive side due to strong Golf tourism in this area. A great spot to set yourself up is the Surf Experience Surf camp at Lagos run by Dago Lipke father of European Junior Champ Marlon Lipke. A pretty cool place to hang out anyway.

There are countless waves in Europe from Ireland to the Iceriver in Munich. Get out there and find your favourite place to fall in love with. Like us you may find that you keep coming back to a particular area year after year and still discover something new and exciting every time you go there.

3 USA and Hawaii

The United States is one of the surfing Meccas of the world. This is where you can surf on 8,000 km of beaches on the west and east coast of the mainland, including Alaska, and above all the 50th State – Hawaii. In Hawaii you will find the famous waves of Waimea, Pipeline or Sunset Beach. In California you surf the waves of Trestles, Rincon, Malibu and Mavericks. Let's go surfing USA.

The West Coast

The west coast of the USA has waves all year round. In summer, southerly swells reach the coast and in winter the northerly swells produce some of the biggest waves around. The best time is usually autumn or fall. In many places you will find kelp floating on the water surface making it smooth glassy often all day long. Surf spots can be found all along the whole coastline. California has the best-known spots, and is recognised still as the origin of surf culture. Its coast has the greatest surfing population in the world. You will meet surfers here from all walks of life. You will find countless surf shops, surfing magazines, surf forecasts and so on and so forth, like nowhere else on the surfing planet. The whole American surfing industry is based in California. A complete industry has been built up around the sport of surfing, and finding a secret spot here is like finding a vacant taxi in New York, a miracle. Nevertheless, there are some great waves and the level of skill in the water is often mind blowing.

The best way to explore the waves of California is to rent a car or buy one, and drive slowly up or down the coastline. You will find value for money motels and fast-food chains on each and every corner.

California has so many surf spots that to try to describe each one would take up a completely new book. Again, the Stormrider guide (North America) is the book of choice to find out more details. For now we just want to name a few highlight on the coast.

We will begin our journey in San Diego and end up in San Francisco under the Golden Gate Bridge. The first spot worth naming is Windansea in La Jolla, a part of San Diego town. Here you will find a peak breaking on a stony sea bottom with a hollow left and right, and a pretty lively local scene. We go on further in the direction of Blacks. A steep, hollow wave that produces nice tubes when the swell is up and the wind is blowing in the right direction. This place sits at the foot of the steep coastline between San Diego and Encinitas, and can be a little tricky to find.

The next stop is Swami's at the entrance of Encinitas. There is a good peak breaking on a sandy bottom dotted with rocks. By the way, Encinitas is also the home of two good friends, Benno and Jeano. With a great eye for detail, they have brought the legendary, classic style Beachcruiser surf-bike to life again under the brand name Electra. Check them out in their shop in Leucadia. Of course, both of them also know where the best waves are, so a visit can be well worthwhile in more then one sense.

The journey goes on past San Onofre directly to Trestles – one of the most famous spots in California. Just before you drive into San Clemente, you have to park your

Californian surf Tom Curren legend of the eigthies

(Photo: Rick Doyle Photography)

car and take a long track down to the beach. There are two waves – one called Upper Trestles and the other Lower Trestles. Both are excellent waves and Trestles is usually packed with people. On towards Los Angeles, you come to Newport with its many stone piers, which tend to create good sandbanks. Newport has some of the best beach breaks that you will find in California.

"Surf City", Huntington Beach, lies next door to Newport. Directly below Huntington Pier is where the best waves are breaking and the legendary Op Pro used to be held here in front of thousands of spectators. The Curren vs. Occilupo battles of the 80 remain unforgettable. Unfortunately also the ugly riots of the OP Pro in 1986. In Los Angeles itself, a surfer shouldn't waste much time. A day is enough to do the standard tourist thing. Sunset Boulevard, Melrose Road, Beverly Hills, Hollywood, Venice Beach and – come on let's get out of here! Just behind LA you will find Malibu, one of the most legendary surfspots in the world. This is where the surfing culture began in the '60s. Surfers, such as Micky Dora, riding the Malibu waves with their large longboards (today called Malibu boards) and developing a super cool style in and out of the water, became surfing legends here.

Today it is difficult to catch a wave in Malibu without at least 10 other surfers already being on it. Onwards, past Oxnard, infamous for its stupid localism – where vandalised boards and car break-ins were quite common – you reach Rincon the most well-known and best point break in California. This is where 80's legend Tom Curren grew up surfing. Going north from Rincon the water gets colder, the waves larger and the crowds smaller. On the road towards San Francisco, it is worthwhile stopping off for a surf-check in Morro Bay, Monterey and Santa Cruz. Here will find a spot called Steamer Lane (notorious for sharks and locals), which lies directly at the foot of a cliff. Everywhere around here you will find a good mixture of point and beach breaks and cold water. Your way now leads to Half Moon Bay and a spot called Mavericks, one of the ultimate big-wave spots on this planet. The tragic death of the Hawaiian big wave expert Mark Foo here in the winter of 94/95 has made this spot additionally legendary. Mark Foo was killed here on a relatively – for Mavericks – "small" day in 18-foot waves. In winter, the best big-wave riders meet here to battle the 20 to 30-foot waves of Mavericks. The local legend, a guy called Jeff Clark surfed the

Mavericks monsters for many years by himself (!) before the surf media and the rest of the world become aware of this awesome wave. Without a doubt, California is one of the best surfing regions in the world, and cruising up and down its coast is definitely worth just like the Beach Boys have been telling us for all those years.

Hawaii

Hawaii – the mention of the name simply, and justifiably, lets the adrenaline level rise in every surfer. Hawaii is the surfing nirvana, the crème de la crème, numero uno, No.1. Got it? The surfing season lasts the whole year round. The islands are open to swells from all directions. The State of Hawaii consists of eight islands, one of which is called Hawaii. The main surfing islands are Oahu, Maui, Kauai and Hawaii itself. The dream island for surfers, however, is Oahu with its capital Honolulu. The best waves of Hawaii break on Oahu's famous North Shore. If you go to Hawaii as a surfer, the North Shore of Oahu is where you want to be. On this short 20 km strip of coast you will find all the legendary waves such as Pipeline, Sunset Beach, Waimea Bay, Haleiwa etc. There is no other place in the world that has so many famous and different waves over such a short stretch.

You can surf on Oahu in summer as well as winter. In summer the breaks on the South Shore of the island come alive. The waves are generated by groundswells coming from the southern hemisphere. The surf is good but rather inconsistent. The South Shore, where Honolulu also sits, is known by the locals as "Town", while the North Shore is called "Country". A well-known surfing company has adopted this as its trade mark – "Town & Country".

Around Honolulu there are several surf spots. Ala Moana Bowl, a big left-handed tube off Ala Moana Beach Park and also other popular spots like Kaisers, Populars, the famous longboard cruiser waves of Waikiki-beach, and last but not least Suicides and Lighthouse off Diamond Head. The real reason why surfers go to Hawaii is the winter wonderland on the North Shore. During winter huge swells come rolling in to the Hawaiian Islands from the north and northwest. Storms in the north Pacific create large swells that sometimes run for thousands of miles until they crash down onto the Hawaiian reefs. These storms bring the famous North Shore of Oahu to life for five months of the year. Particularly in December there is hardly another place on earth where you will find so many hot surfers in one spot. The season lasts from November to March. For mere mortals it is advisable to avoid the main season in December, unless of course you want to watch the Pipeline Masters (one of the most spectacular contests in professional surfing). During this time the waves are gigantic and the water is packed with professional surfers as the pro tour ends and the world champion is crowned. It can be hard to find a bed to sleep in during the peak season. Apart from the crowds, the waves can easily get too big for the average surfer. We therefore recommend that you visit Hawaii from January onwards. The pros have left, and you will be able to find accommodation, and the raging ocean will calm down at least somewhat. Despite being the back end of the season you do not need to be afraid that there will be no waves left for you. When you are on the plane at the end you will go home knowing that you will have ridden some of the biggest waves in your surfing life. The waves rarely drop below 6 feet at this time of year. The waves in Hawaii are very powerful, and you will certainly need at least a seven-foot board or even a few inches longer if the surf is on.

International flights all land in Honolulu. Get ready to be shocked when you see famous Waikiki Beach – thousands of tourists on a small stretch of sand with a concrete jungle as a backdrop. Did someone say paradise? It is an American big city, just like any other.

High season on the North Shore

(Photo: joli)

The best thing to do is to hire a car and drive out to the North Shore. The drive will take about 45 minutes, and you can find good accommodation once you get there. Surf shops as well as the main super market Foodland, which is located just behind Waimea Bay and known to be the most expensive supermarket in the US, often have a black-board with classified including private lodgings. When we were there we found a cheap but nice room costing US $10 a day per person this way. An alternative is the Back-packers Hostel, which used to belong to big wave legend Mark Foo before he drowned at Mavericks in California. You will find this directly behind Waimea Bay as you come from the direction of Haleiwa. A dormitory bed here will cost you around US $15.

There are a lot of great waves on the North Shore. To start with you should buy yourself a surf guide book from one of the surf shops. We recommend the "Surfer's Guide to Hawaii" by Greg Ambrose. It has all the details about currents, sea bottoms, best wind and swell directions etc. It also covers the islands of Maui, Kauai and Hawaii. We just want to take a quick look at a few of the main spots on the North Shore. The surfing wonderland starts directly on Haleiwa Alií Beach Park. The waves break on a stony bottom and give you a quick, sometimes hollow, right-hander and a short left-hander. When the swell is big Haleiwa is a pretty heavy wave, in addition the current can be very strong and will rather unusually pull you away from the shoulder right onto the peak. So sitting on the shoulder and watching it for a while before you tackle your first wave can be tricky. Take a comfortable little drive down the North Shore over Haleiwa Bridge and past Surf n Sea surf shop and stop at Laniakea. This is a great right reef-break with many hollow sections allowing rides of up to 400 metres. Being able to check the waves from your car is a bonus. Keep driving until you get to a gap between the houses and trees blocking the view to the surf. You have arrived at Jocko's and Chun's, which are right next to each other divided by a deep-water channel. Jocko's is a fast and hollow left-hander, which delivers everything from 4-foot fun waves to pitching 10-footers. Chun's reef has one of the easiest waves on the North Shore and is therefore popular with North Shore first timers as well as Longboarders. It is mainly a right but there is also a short left. Chun's can handle waves from 2 to 8 feet and is the perfect place to get to know the North Shore. Two days here and you are ready to move on. The next stop brings you to the No. 1 big-wave spot – Waimea Bay. The waves here are really only for the experts. Just stand on the cliff and watch the spectacle (i.e. at the yearly held Eddie Aikau contest). With anything up to ten surfers on one 30-foot wave, this is no place for you. This is serious stuff and many people have been hurt, some have died here. So keep your fingers off and just watch! Driving past spots like Rockpile

Banzaiii!

Pipeline, Hawaii just awesome

(Photos: Menges & Diel)

and Log Cabins, you will soon get to one of the most famous and dangerous waves in the world. Directly opposite the Sunset Beach Elementary School is where you find it – the "Banzai Pipeline". This is the ultimate left-hand tube. The right-hander on the same wave is called "Backdoor" and is by no means any less awesome. Pipeline or "Pipe" is the benchmark for all other tubes around the world. It breaks onto a reef in extremely shallow water close to the beach. You cannot afford to make any mistakes here. A wipe-out in big waves often ends with a serious injury and some deaths have occurred as well. No doubt without the absolutely hard-core lifeguards always keeping a watchful eye over the break, many more people would have died here over the years. The impact zone is lethal so forget duck-diving. Wiping out or getting caught inside at Pipe is a nightmare. Pipeline breaks from between 4 to 20 feet. At 12 feet plus it starts breaking further out on the so-called second reef. No matter how often you have seen the wave in pictures or on video, nothing can prepare you for the real thing. Pipe is not the place for big manoeuvres; it is all about tube, big square tubes. A long drop, a huge barrel and maybe a quick cutback at the end, that's it. Sounds easy, looks easy however it is anything but easy. Even the Hawaiians or the Pros will never play this wave down as they too do get hurt here. At the end of December the "Pipemasters" take place here – the last competition of the year and often the showdown for the World Title. Moving on past Rocky Point, a high performance peak with a left and a right-hander, you arrive at the third jewel of the North Shore – Sunset Beach with its sensational and awesome right-hander. After a big steep drop and a flatter middle section there is a thick tube on the inside called "Inside Sunset". Sunset breaks some 800 metres out to sea from between 4 to 20 feet. You can easily paddle out through a channel. But watch out for the notorious west peaks. They often break right across the channel. Everyone will get caught inside at Sunset one day or the other. If you do get caught and lose your board (which you often will) swim in towards the beach with the waves and the white water and avoid swimming towards the very tempting, calm channel. Coming in with the breaking waves you will obviously receive some serious punishment, however swim-ming in through the channel is virtually impossible due to the strong current. About 1 km after Sunset beach you reach Velzeyland. Mainly a righthander, that used to be locals only but is pretty much open to everyone showing a bit of respect these days. V-Land breaks between 3 to 8 feet and also works as a smaller reform on those humun-gous 30 ft days. That's it, you have reached the end of the North Shore. How long did that take? 25 minutes? It is unbelievable how many great spots lie along this short stretch. So let's turn around and start all over again.

If you stop anywhere along the North Shore to go surfing, do not leave any valuables in the car. Unfortunately we had to learn this lesson ourselves by having a video camera (with some good footage on it) stolen once. The surf check in Hawaii is crucial. Take a good look at where you will enter the water and where other surfers exit it and never underestimate the size and power of the waves when you check them from the safety of the beach. Always remember that conditions in Hawaii can change very rapidly. You paddle out to some 6-foot waves, and three sets later they are already coming in at 8-foot. Sometimes the swell size can double within an hour. If you are in Hawaii during the main season, there will often be days when the waves are too big for the average surfer. Just sit back and watch and enjoy the spectacle. Soon the swell will drop and you will be able to ride clean and very achievable 6-8 ft waves and no doubt you will score some unbelievable rides.

In Hawaii, the local scene is very, very lively, and, as a non-Hawaiian, you should stay clear of some spots e.g., Makaha on the Westside. The locals, some of them organised in gangs called "Da Hui" or "the Wolfpack" demand respect, otherwise things can easily get violent. So behave well, carry plenty of smiles and wait for your turn when you are in the water. Treat the locals with the respect they deserve and you will receive some of the Aloha spirit in return.

The other islands also offer some great surfing, particularly Maui. This island is actually better known for its windsurfing, particularly at Hookipa Beach. The best waves in Maui are at Honolua Bay in the north of the island, with a long peeling, right-hand point break which works from 3 to 20-foot. Another wave, called Peahi, better known as "Jaws", has become the hot spot for tow-in surfing in mega waves. In tow surfing, the surfer is towed behind a jetski like a water skier and pulled into waves of a size and speed that he would otherwise not have been able to paddle into. Tow surfers use specially designed boards with foot straps or bindings to avoid being bounced off at high speed. Surfers such as Laird Hamilton, Dave Kalama and Buzzy Kerbox to name just some of the pioneers with their combination of surfing and windsurfing skills, have opened a new dimension of big or rather monster wave surfing. At Jaws, waves in the 30 to 40 foot range have successfully been ridden. Who knows what else is possible?

Hawaii is a real paradise if you stay away from Honolulu and it is definitely well worth a trip or two or three. So better start practicing holding your breath in the bath. Aloha!

4 Australia

Australia, Down-under, Oz, or however you call it, is a dreamland for every surfer. The whole east coast with spots like the Superbank, Lennox Head, Aussie Pipe and Bells, the south coast with Cactus, and the west coast with Margret River and the Box make this place, kilometre after kilometre, and spot after spot, an absolute surfers' paradise. You can surf on a city beach of a 4 million people metropolis or surf in total isolation in the middle of the West Australian desert. The main focus however, is on the east coast with its centres of population in Melbourne, Sydney and Brisbane. It is highly likely that you will make your first contact with Australian waves somewhere along here because this is where the best-known and easy to find spots are. However, the great variety of waves is really the fascinating thing about surfing in Australia.

In Australia you will always find a protected bay or peninsula where there are clean waves breaking in a sheltered area. Although wintertime can deliver some real monster waves at places like "Ours" the surf in Australia is typically in the 4-6ft range and rarely gets over 10 feet.

Nevertheless, even at 6 ft some of the waves can be pretty gnarly, particularly some of the reefbreaks. You will have to get used to enter and exit the water over rocks and the like as many waves break near cliffs or rocks. A thorough surf check is always a must.

The planning for your journey will naturally be dependent on the season of the year. In the Australian winter (June to October), the swells come up from the south and from the west. Southern Australia, Western Australia as well as the southern east coast have cold but powerful waves during this time. Although the climate cannot exactly be called a real winter, a full suit will be necessary.

In summer (November to February), the Australians often struggle with small waves and onshore winds. However, the odd summer swell is also possible. Moving out of summer in the period between February to April the cyclone season starts. Just off the far northeast coast, areas of low-pressure build up and create so-called cyclones. If you ever lucky enough to catch a cyclone swell, you will never forget it. From Brisbane down to around Sydney, the whole east coast turns it on. While you will find the most perfect waves at the famous spots such as the Superbank or Burleigh Heads, hundreds of bays and beaches along the east coast are capable of delivering all-time waves during a cyclone swell. As a bonus you will not need a lot of rubber on you because the water is still at a comfortable temperature from summer. It is essential to get your hands on a good surf guidebook that will tell you under what conditions which spots are working and where to find them. In our view, one of the best books we have come across in this respect is the "Surfing and Sailboarding Guide to Australia" by Nat Young. The edition we have is rather old, and we are not sure whether it is still in print. But there are many other books to choose from. One, which, beside good information, also has lots of great photos, is "Mark Warren's Surf Guide to Australia".

For your first surfing trip we suggest the following itinerary: take a flight towards the end of January to Sydney, buy or hire a car, rattle around the Sydney area for a few days, and then head north up the coast. On your way north you will pass some of the most beautiful beaches and incredibly picturesque surf spots. We recommend this itinerary because we think that if you are a newcomer to Australia

True Aussie locals dropping in

(Photo: Kelly Smith, Smico. Surfer: Leigh Sedley)

it offers all you have been dreaming about: sun, warm water and great waves. On a second trip to Australia, you should give the uncrowded power waves of the Australian winter or autumn in Victoria or Southern Australia a try, or go on a surfari in the lonely region of Western Australia. There are countless options. Just like Arnold Schwarzenegger says in Terminator I, "I'll be back".

Localism can be an issue in particular at some of the more well-known spots, and whilst not as intimidating as say in Hawaii, the locals do demand respect. This said the general vibe in Australia is very friendly and open towards tourists and newcomers. There is a group of locals, however, that are better not messed with: the notorious sharks. In Australia there are many sharks, but they only present a danger in rare cases. Above all it is the loners – the white shark and the tiger shark – that are a threat to humans in the colder waters of Southern and Western Australia. Here, any intruder in their stamping ground is considered to be potential food. The smaller types of shark live mostly in groups or swarms and generally have something better to do than attack such a large animal as the human being. If you want to play it safe, do not go surfing at dawn or dusk as it is dinner time at Mr. and Mrs. Shark's. If you spot a shark in the water, take the next wave surfing in the prone position to avoid falling off in all nervousness. Counting all our trips together, we have probably spent more than three years in Australia, sometimes surfing in some out-of-the-way places, but we have only ever seen sharks in the water twice. The men in the grey suits were somehow much more interested in the ten million other fish in the water. On closer examination many fins cutting through the water surface turned out to be non other than our friend 'Flipper', who is quite common in Australia, and who loves to join the surfers in the water.

Bon appetit!

(Drawing: Stefan "Muli" Müller)

Victoria (March–October)

In Australian slang, "Victoria" means "big, powerful waves" (just kidding). You should look for these in winter and autumn along what is called the "Great Ocean Road" starting in a town called Torquay. Torquay is the surfing head office of Australia – the base and origin of many big surf brands like Rip Curl or Quiksilver. Stock up on any sort of surf equipment in one of the mega surfshops and outlets. Next to Torquay is famous Bells Beach with its long big walls and the legendary surfing championships at Easter. But it is not only Bells that gets the adrenaline flowing. Virtually next door you have another world class wave called Winkipop. In any case, the whole area around Torquay and all the way up the Great Ocean Road is full of good waves. Seek and you shall find!

New South Wales (All Year Round)

The centre of NSW is Sydney. Although it is a big city with millions of people, there are some beautiful beaches and quality surf spots. The well-known spots are Manly, Bondi and in particular North Narabeen. Narabeen is north of Sydney and has produced numerous world famous surfers. The main surf spot is at the northern end of the beach – hence the name. It is only a beach break, but the quality of the waves can be pretty high. But since it is still a city beach, it is usually very crowded, and has a firm, laid-down pecking order: the locals on top and the tourists underneath. Further north are Freshwater and Avalon (reef breaks). You can simply drive along the shoreline and check all the spots, one after the other. However, before your journey takes you further up north, you should spend a few days on the south coast of NSW south of Sydney. Start from the industrial town of Wollongong about an hour south from Sydney. A stop here is well worth it, not just because of the waves around Wollongong (Woonona and Sandon Point are a couple of names for you to start with). If you need a new board or some other equipment, you should check out the surf shop run by the Byrne brothers. Two of the brothers are former pro surfers, the third, Phil Byrne, is a shaper who became famous for making Tom Caroll's world championship boards and is still today carving out boards for many Australia pros. The brothers not only sell top-class boards, they are also happy to help you find the best waves in the area. As soon

"High" skills around Sydney

(Photo: Kelly Smith, Smico, Surfer: Micro Copa)

as you leave Wollongong behind, you start to encounter the breathtaking unspoiled nature of the south coast with kangaroos, colourful birds and everything that goes with it in particular surf spot after surf spot.

The Australian Pipeline or "Aussie Pipe" is worth a special mention. The spot is situated near an indigenous community, and the locals definitely have the final say in the water. If you do not show respect, you will soon be sent back to the beach. Leave the waves to the locals where they want them and you will be rewarded with a great session. This left-hander breaks perfectly and the tube is almost always open. Getting there is a bit of a challenge: About 15 km south of Nowra is the turn off to Jervis Bay. Follow this road to Wreck Bay. Somewhere along the route you will come across the signpost "Summercloud Bay", which you follow. Park the car (makes sure to leave no valuables behind) and then walk through the bush for about 20 minutes until you reach the beach. Take a good look at the entry and exit points as this will save you a few cuts and bruises getting in and out over the sharp, sea urchin invested reef.

Eventually back up in Sydney just keep heading north along the Pacific Highway. Water and weather get warmer the further you go north. All along the route you will find many known and unknown top-class surf spots.

You should definitely make a stop at Crescent Head (long right-hand point break and a cool local pub with good food) as well as further north at Yamba. Just outside Yamba is Angourie Point. This is a beautiful stretch of land in a national park with superb waves in particular at the Point. By the way, the entry into the water at the tip of the peninsula can be pretty hairy in big surf. Good timing and avoiding slipping or stumbling on the slippery ground when you race into the water between sets is important.

The next world-class wave on your way northwards is the right-hander at Lennox Head. This is one of the many point breaks in Australia where a good wave here is worth twenty elsewhere. But take care, the waves break on an unforgiving rock bottom.

From here it is only a few kilometres to Byron Bay – the pilgrimage destination of backpackers from all around the world. There is a lot going on here, not only in the local bars but definitely also out in the surf. During the 70s Byron Bay was the favourite spot for many surfers, who sought an alternative lifestyle, surf all day and "live off the land". The best known wave in the area is the long right-hand point break called the "Pass", directly on the southern end of the large bay. You cannot miss it. The water is warm and the waves are long and open.

From here it is only a stone's throw north to the Queensland border, the next state full of waves.

Queensland (October to April)

Queensland begins north of the Tweed River, and the action starts right at the border. The southern part of Queensland is also called the Gold Coast, which besides being the home of some of the best point breaks in the world is notorious for its raging night life. If you ever experience a cyclone swell here, you will wake up at night for the rest of your live stammering the words "Superbank, Burleigh, ... Party".

Duranbah is one of the best beach breaks in Australia and lies directly next to the rivermouth of the Tweed River. The standard of surfing in the water is extremely high. It is that high that even some of the professionals who live here do not stand out particularly. This beach break can really fire and offers everything from sand dredging barrels to aerial launch pad.

Just over the hill are the famous Queensland point breaks around the town of Coolangatta. Starting with Snapper Rocks it connects directly into Rainbow Bay and Greenmount. They used to be three separate spots but due to sand being dredged out of the Tweed River mouth and deposited near shore at Snapper Rocks the so called Superbank was created. The name says almost everything. It is a loooooong, barrelling, perfect wave. However due to the changes in sand deposits along the coast, one of the best barrels in the world Kirra Point, a little further north, as well as Greenmount got lost in the process. This means that where people use to be able to choose from 4 different breaks the attention is now all on the Superbank starting at Snapper Rocks breaking into Rainbow Bay. The crowd factor can be hilarious during peak season and that is really not all that "Super". When the Superbank is on, it is not uncommon to see a round 100 surfers in the water, at 5 o'clock in the morning!

This does not mean that it is impossible to catch a wave. Since the wave is seemingly endless, you can wait further down the line for the opportunity that a surfer will not make the tube or will fall off during a manoeuvre. This strategy is not such a bad one because the outside, where the wave begins to break, is usually filled up by locals

Point Breaks galore in Queensland

(Photo: Kelly Smith, Smico. Surfer: Jay "Bottle" Thompson)

who know the wave inside out. Be careful when you start further down the line though. The locals are real masters of the tube and often, just when it seems that the surfer will never make it out of the tube, he proves you wrong and comes flying out of the barrel. So, do not take-off unless you are 200% sure that the surfer has wiped-out. Unfortunately, at the Superbank you cannot expect that any priority rules will be obeyed. Drop-ins by locals and tourist alike are common. There is no need to be upset and excited about this. Surf the wave until eventually someone will drop-in you. Usually your ride will be at least three times as long as your average beach break wave anyway. Paddle back out without engaging in any major disputes. It is just not worth it. Up to you if you want to pay back the villain at the next occasion. A further 20 minutes along the coast you will arrive at the next Australian classic, Burleigh Heads. Just another world-class right-hand point break, which offers long clean tubes on a sandy bottom. When the swell is big, Burleigh is generally better than the Superbank. Despite its sandy bottom, you should not underestimate this wave and there is a strong down-the-line current running through the line-up.

Past the casino and party-town "Surfer's Paradise" (no joke, this is really the name of this town, and there actually are some pretty good beach breaks), you go in the direction of Noosa Heads – a further Ausssie highlight. The scenery is lush and tropical, and in the Noosa Heads National Park you will once again find long and clean right hand point break waves. In the right conditions Noosa can be one of the best waves in Australia.

Before leaving this continent we do not want to forget Australia's own version of Teahupoo or Godzilla for that matter. On Tasmania, another Australian state situated actually on an island south of the mainland, you will find a place called Shipsterns. We mention it not because we want you to go and surf it. We just mentioned it so the next time you watch a surfmovie with some lunatic dropping into a 12 foot, totally unmakeble looking monster, negotiating a 4 foot step halfway down the face before being sucked into one of the heaviest barrels on this earth you will know where this thing is at home. Tasmania has cold water and empty clean waves. Definitely a place to visit if you want to enjoy some untouched nature and get away from it all.

Travelling up and down and around Australia you will discover a new spot, which only works under particular conditions, every time you go. Reason enough to turn yourself into a human boomerang that keeps coming back. See you later mate!

5 South Pacific

The islands of the South Pacific are one the most beautiful parts of this world. After our trip through this region, we perfectly understood why there was a Mutiny on the Bounty when they were sailing in these waters. Our own tour took us through Fiji, the Cook Islands and Tahiti. However, the other island groups such as Tonga or Samoa also have fantastic waves. If you do not want to discover the islands on your own, you can book a boat charter or stay in one of the many tropical surf resorts. Bookings are easy through the standard surf travel companies like Worldsurfaris.com or Wavehunters.com. The best time for a trip to the South Pacific is between April and October. The swells are created by storms in the Tasmanian Sea, the Coral Sea and Antarctica.

Fiji

Going to Fiji, you will only have one wave in your mind – "Cloudbreak". Truly one of the best lefts in the world. Every year, loads of surfers from all over the world come to Fiji just to ride this wave. Like "Pipeline" in Hawaii, surfers always speak in awe of this wave. We are certainly able to confirm this: after two weeks – with a group of just ten surfers, we had ten broken boards, a broken arm, broken leashes galore, dings all over our boards and countless more or less serious reef cuts. "Cloudbreak" is a powerful and fast hollow left reef break. The wave breaks in the middle of the ocean on a shallow coral reef, and can only be reached by boat. If you want to surf any of the classic breaks of the main island Viti Levu, you must book ahead as the surf camps have and enforce exclusivity of the breaks for their well-paying guests. Tavarua islands provides access to Cloudbreak and Restaurants and Namotu surf resort to the reef directly in front of the island. Obviously, this concept of exclusive surf rights is highly controversial, but at this point in time there is simply no other way then to go with it and pay top dollar to ride these waves. The resorts themselves offer quality yet not luxurious accommodation in a dream-like setting and cater entirely for the surfers needs. For about US $ 200 per day, you live full-board with meals and boat transfers to the breaks included. There are other waves in the area as well without the exclusive access rights, but they too are only accessible by boat.

International flights all land in Nadi on Viti Levu. Your accommodation provider will usually pick you up from the airport. You do not need a car on Fiji. Once on the resort islands, a boat will take you out to the break and anchor in the channel while you surf your brains out. "Cloudbreak" is a radical wave. It breaks onto a flat reef shelf and can provide rides up to 200 metres. When the wave hits the reef, the lip pitches forward at least as far as the wave is high.

The feeling when you make the drop and the massive lip crashes down on the reef just next to you is hard to describe in words. Pure adrenaline! If you wipe-out, you are immediately in trouble. You are likely to hit the sharp reef and after being thrown around you quickly find yourself standing in only knee-deep water with the next wave about to hit you. There is no duck-diving as the water now is far too shallow. At this point you are at the mercy of the waves. Just do the starfish and let the waves wash you sideways into the channel, and be thankful when you escape with only a few scratches. Taking the first wave of a set is not a good idea,

Cloudbreak, Fiji

(Photo: Jeff Hornbaker, Quiksilver)

because if you do not make it, the next wave in the set will mercilessly eat you alive. One tricky thing about Cloudbreak is that unless you ride the wave to its very end (e.g. if you only want to surf a particular section of the wave) there is a good chance that your are still going to get caught by a bigger set following suit. The channel however is relatively safe, and even if the waves are too big for you to surf, you should paddle out and just sit on the shoulder for a while. You will surely receive the biggest adrenaline rush of your life when you feel and see the power and size of these waves from close up. Besides that, you will never forget the picture of a surfer standing tall with outstretched arms in the biggest tube you have ever seen. Keep your wits sharp, however, for the notorious boomer-sets that swing wide will knock you off the shoulder. Even on smaller days Cloudbreak is a world-class wave as it breaks with unbelievable perfection.

If you have the time and the necessary change, do go to Fiji. Besides the fantastic waves you will meet some of the friendliest people on this planet. The Fijians take things pretty easy. They have their own time − Fiji time and a local drink called Cava which is actually a weak narcotic and tastes like mud. Fijians are never in a hurry as everything goes a little slowly here. The most important word to learn on Fiji is "Bula". Greet everyone you meet with a friendly Bula. It means simply "Hello" and is sure to bring the biggest smiles to the faces of the locals. So, on that note "Bula, Bula!"

Tahiti

Tahiti is the picture-perfect South Pacific paradise. These French-Polynesian islands look like everything you would imagine about paradise: white sand, blue lagoons, dolphins and perfect waves. The best known islands for surfing are Tahiti itself, Moorea and Huahine. Huahine has one of the very few right-handers in the French-Polynesian island group. However, the local scene is rumoured to be a bit of a worry and does not particularly welcome the surfing tourists, hence we decided to go elsewhere and focus on the other two islands. The most famous spot on the main island is Teahupoo or Chopes, which these days is featured in every surf magazine and movie with its gnarly, grinding monster tubes. If "Pipeline" in Hawaii is starting to feel a bit boring, try Teahupoo to get the blood pressure up again. The town of Teahupoo sits near the southwest corner of the smaller of Tahiti's two dormant volcanoes, Tahiti Iti. Make no mistake, this is a serious and life

(Rider: Raimana, Spot: Teahupoo, Tahiti
Photo: Tim McKenna, Billabong)

Insane!

Teahupoo

threatening wave that only the best surfers can ride successfully. People have died here being caught inside or wiping out. In the year 2000 Laird Hamilton was towed into and rode a monster wave that at the time was truly the heaviest wave ever surfed.

Moorea has some slightly less radical, but equally perfect waves. The islands get their swells from the Antarctic storms, which come up from the southwest.

Prices on Tahiti are, however, anything but cheap. For a simple night's stay you will easily have to pay well above US $ 50. A hire car will cost you a quick US $ 100 a day. You cannot even get a pizza for less than US $ 15. The main town of Papeete is particularly dear. It is enough if you spend the first and last night there. Our tip, unless you are there to look at or surf Teahupoo, is to hop on the ferry to Moorea, which departs several times a day. One of the best waves in the region – the left-hand reef at Haapiti – breaks on Moorea. Apart from the many luxury resorts, a few hundred metres past the Club Med, there is also a backpackers hostel and a camping ground, still not exactly cheap, but there is not much else to choose from.

Moorea has about six spots, of which Haapiti is the Number 1. The town of Haapiti sits roughly in the middle of the west side of the island. The break is not easy to find though.

Look out for a small concrete landing pier built out into the water. From there it is about a half-an-hour's paddle over the lagoon to the reef passage that the wave breaks into. It is not unusual to have dolphins accompany you across the lagoon. If you are really lucky a local may even give you a lift in his boat which saves a lot of paddling. Just before you reach the reef passage a current will pull you out to sea. On your trip to the South Pacific, in general it is a good idea to bring a pair of binoculars with you so that you can at least see and somewhat estimate the wave size from shore. At Haapiti, you will be surprised how big the waves actually are when you are across the lagoon and are coming closer to the reef. Haapiti works in a southwest swell and from 4 to 12 feet. French-Polynesia is an amazing but expensive paradise. If you accept this fact and budget for it, you will have a great time surfing some of the bluest and cleanest barrels in the world.

6 Indonesia

Indonesia consists of about 12,000 islands with countless waves. Most surfers however go to Bali. Since the 70s, Bali attracts surfing (and other) tourists from all over the world, above all Australians, as it is really just around the corner for them. Over the last years, the more adventurous have more and more explored the other islands to get away from the crowds in Bali. Numerous new spots have been discovered, and surf camps have sprung up everywhere. For an excellent overview over the whole region and its waves, including Bali, we recommend "Surfing Indonesia" by Leonard and Lorca Lueras (Periplus Action Guides) and the all-time classic "Indo Surf & Lingo". It contains pretty much all you need to know about the Indonesian surf spots, some information about culture and the most useful Indonesian words. English, by the way, does not get you very far outside of Bali.

Bali

Let's head to Bali for a start. The dry season begins in May and ends in September. During this time the action is on the west side of Bali, particularly the famous waves of Uluwatu and Padang Padang on the so-called Bukit Peninsula. The waves are created by big low pressure systems far off in the deep Indian Ocean. On top of that, during this time, the prevailing winds are from the southeast which create offshore conditions that often last the whole day. On a good day you will find anywhere between 50-100 surfers in the water at Uluwatu. To get away from these crowds you will have to go to other Indonesian islands like for example the islands of Java and Sumatra to the west, or the easterly islands such as Lombok, Sumbawa or West Timor, or even sail through the Mentawai islands off Sumatra.

The rainy season, on the other hand, often brings big waves and offshore conditions from west winds on the east side of Bali, mainly known for its numerous luxury resorts. During this time the main breaks are Sanur and Nusa Dua. This season begins in December and ends around early March. On Bali the choice is all yours. For example you can surf beach breaks, only a few though, around Kuta and Legian. If you are looking for reef breaks, you can have razor-sharp ones, extremely shallow ones and deeper, not so dangerous ones. In Bali, you can surf waves from 2 to around 12 feet. You do not have to necessarily stick to the main seasons mentioned above to find good conditions. The transition periods between the dry and rainy seasons also produce good waves, but the weather can be somewhat inconsistent. People say that there is always at least a 2-footer breaking somewhere on Bali.

In the dry season, Kuta is the place to stay. Here you can always find a reasonably priced hotel, and buy a great meal like grilled fish with lots of garlic for around US $ 5. There are all sorts of things to do in the evening; play pool, watch surfing videos in one of the many bars such as the legendary "Tubes". Unfortunately late night parties often have the side effect of missing the early morning sessions, which for this very reason are often the least crowded and therefore best ones. Kuta itself is really far from an exotic paradise these days. Despite all the changes (often to the worse) the waves in Bali have stayed the same. You will usually fly into Bali's main Airport called Denpassar (the capital of Bali) but which is actually just outside of Kuta. The best thing is to get a taxi

Empty perfection in Bali

(Photo: Menges/Diel)

and let it take you directly into town and look for a hotel near the beach and the airport. Here you will have several Surf spots directly on your doorstep. Just next to the Airport runway, built out into the water, there are the two quality spots Airport Rights and Lefts. You can get tubed while the jumbos thunder through the sky above you. If you prefer a beach break to adjust to the conditions in Bali, you can try the waves at Kuta Beach (e.g. "Halfways" in front of the Rama Palace Hotel) and Legian Beach. These are actually pretty good beach breaks with sometimes clean and hollow conditions.

Apart from a few quality reef breaks in Kuta, the best waves are in the south of Bali, about an hour from Kuta on the so-called Bukit Peninsula. It is therefore important to hire a car or a motorcycle in Kuta. The best-known wave on Bali, Uluwatu, is in the south near the temple with the same name. Next to this are two spots Padang Padang (double because double good and heavy) and Bingin. All three waves are extremely fast, hollow and break in shallow water over a sharp reef bottom. To get to Uluwatu you have to head south past the Airport and follow the signs to the Uluwatu temple. You will pass several handwritten "surf" signposts and finally get to the turn off that takes you to the cliff top at Ulu's. These days there is a luxury resort right on top of the cliff overlooking the break. Just follow everyone down the cliff and pick one of the many Warungs built into the cliff as your base for the day. Usually you can safely leave all you gear behind in "your" Warung when you go for a surf. After your session you can spoil yourself with basic but delicious food (nasi goring and fruit salad are recommended) and cool drinks or simply lie down and relax, or get a massage as you watch the other surfers pull into tube after tube. You can also buy basic surf supplies (wax, leash, used boards) at some of the Warungs. To get out into the surf you have to climb down a ladder into a cave at the bottom of the cliff. At low tide you can easily walk out of the cave, but at high tide you will have to paddle out and what is more important belly ride back into the cave. Timing is everything here. Try and aim well before the cave on your final wave so the current takes you towards the entry. If you aim straight for the cave you will usually miss the exit as the strong current sweeps you past it and you will be required to go full circle to the outside, catch another wave and aim right next time. Booties come in very handy at low tide, when you need to walk over the dry reef to get to the waters edge. Uluwatu is not an easy wave, but if you make the drop, race along the wall as the lip flies over your head and you manage to come out of the tube. Everything else, the bumpy road, the crowds and your upset stomach are then forgotten. You will find similar conditions at Padang Padang and Bingin. Padang is somewhat gnarlier and more dangerous and only breaks when the swell is around 6 foot plus i.e., when Uluwatu is maxing out. On Bali, however, the surf is not only dependent on the swell or the wind. It is essential to know the times for high and low tide. Some spots are simply too dangerous to surf when the tide is out and the water extremely shallow.

Finally, a few words about the other Indonesian islands. Above all, two waves have become popular. One is the right-hander on Sorake beach in Lagundri Bay on Nias Island, simply called Nias, which lies just off the coast of Sumatra. Accommodation and food is cheap and the waves are cooking, literally. The water and air temperature is very warm. Malaria can be a problem, so go prepared. The Airport on Nias is at Gunungsitoli and from here it is about another 4 hrs by car or shuttle to Lagundri Bay. Nias was almost completely destroyed during the big Tsunami but it seems as though the surf is now better then ever.

The other dream wave (or nightmare depending on its size) lies on the south-east tip of Java at a place called Garajigang, also known as G-Land. G-Land breaks best during the dry season and works between 4 to 12 feet. It is a kind of left-hand point break/reef break, which runs through four main sections, some of them can really dish out some heavy barrels. G-Land is a perfect but intimidating wave when it is big. As we write this there are two surfcamps in G-Land ("Jungle Village" and "Bobby's Surfcamp"). You can book them either over the web or directly in Kuta at around US $ 350 a week. The camp organisers usually arrange a pick-up from Kuta by boat. Despite their remoteness and somewhat difficult access, both Nias and G-Land can still get crowded, so don't be disappointed as no doubt you will still be able to pull into some smoking hot waves.

Mentawai Islands

Everyone who flicked through a Surf Magazine over the last 5 years or so will have seen pictures off the waves in the Mentawais, the Telos or Hinakos, an island chain just off Sumatra. This is where some of the most perfect waves in the world can be found. The amazing thing is that the conditions you see in the magazines (glassy tubes) are pretty much what you will find once you get there. The Mentawais are simply super-consistent with good swells and low winds if you somewhat stick to the main season from April to October. Of course there is a downside to this as well. If we are able to tell you all this in our book it means unfortunately the Mentwais are anything but a hidden secret. The global Surf industry loads all their sponsored surfers from young guns to seasoned champions on the various boat charters and sometimes simply takes over this paradise to do all their promotion photos and movies. Add a few boat loads of other hotties from around the world and you can easily find yourself stranded on your boat watching but not surfing these perfect waves. Up to ten boats parked near the most well-known spots is not an unusual sight in the main season. The solution is on the one hand to stay away from the busiest months and on the other hand to pick an experienced skipper who will be able to avoid the big name spots like Lances right or Maccaronies. Instead he will be able to find you some more low key spots that break, maybe not quite as perfect as the ones mentioned above, yet still provide some pretty incredible waves, which should be more then enough to create a perfect surf trip for the average surfer.

The other downside is clearly the remoteness of these islands. This is true in more then one sense. Firstly to finally paddle out into the line-up you will have to fly to Singapore, change flights to the city of Padang on the coast of Sumatra, then by car to the harbour, zodiac out to the main boat and then cruise (or bump depending on the swell) overnight across the straight to arrive at the surf the next morning. You do need a fair amount of patience. Secondly, medical help in case of an emergency can be a critical issue. Despite the fact that minor repairs (stitches etc.) can be done by the boat crew the shallow, sharp reefs have plenty of potential to cause some serious damage to your body. The nearest doctor is in Padang which means at least a twelve hour (sometimes bumby) boat ride back to the harbour. Combine that with a broken bone or a major cut you have pretty nasty scenario at hand. Malaria can be a problem even staying on a boat (one of our friends got bitten and subsequently developed malaria while we where anchored near the spot Maccaronies overnight). So precautions, including the latest anti-malaria medication, should be taken. But don't be scared and Carpe Diem because the Mentawais and the other near islands are simply delivering perfection. The relatively soft yet perfect right at Nias, the mega-left Asu and it's right brother Bawa (Hinakos),

Eric hiding from the sun at Maccas

(Photo: Ashton Robinson)

barrels galore at Lances Right (HT's as it is often referred to) or the hotdoggers delight Maccaroni's (Macca's), which 8 times World Champ Kelly Slater called "the funniest left in the world " are simply too good to be missed.

The water in Indonesia is warm so you will not need a wetsuit. Nevertheless, you should pack a wetshirt or rashguard to protect yourself from the strong sun. To make yourself understood you should remember the following two sentences: "Terima kasih" – 'Thank you' or also 'No, thank you' and "Saya cari ombak-ombak besar" – 'I'm looking for big waves'.

Finally a few words about some of the recent incidents in this part of the world: The whole world was shocked when Christmas 2004 a tsunami destroyed parts of Sumatra, Thailand, Sri Lanka, India and the Maldives claiming an almost unspeakable number of lives. Despite the most film footage seen on television stemming from the beaches of Thailand, the region by far the worst affected was the Aceh region in northern Sumatra. Amazingly we had been on a boat charter just 100 km off the epicentre a month before the tsunami. The news hit us like a hammer. What had happened to all the super friendly locals on the islands and what about the boat crews? It soon turned out that most of the Mentawais had been spared and that the boats where OK – at least some relief. However, another tsunami a few months later had a terrible impact on Nias and Lagundri Bay.

We also only missed the terrible Bali nightclub bombings (that killed hundreds of people, many of them surfers) by a month as we spent our final night in Bali in one of the night clubs that were later bombed.

So what is the consequence for a surfer travelling in that part of the world? No doubt Indonesia is a risky destination. Everyone should be clear about the risk involved and it is up to the individual to decide whether it is all worth it. As for us, we will certainly not stop travelling to Indo. On the one hand many poor locals live off the travelling surfers and to stop going there would simply mean the next disaster for them. On the other hand also our daily life in the so-called "civilisation" bears countless risks that are well beyond our control.

Our thoughts go out to all the victims of the terrorist attacks and the natural disasters in South East Asia. A donation to Surf Aid (www.surfaidinternational.org), a non-profitable organisation that focuses its attention on the needs of the Indonesian surf regions with a particular program to help to fight malaria among the locals, should be a definite Nobrainer for all travelling surfers.

Going right on Nias Island

(Photo: Joli)

7 South Africa

South Africa's coasts offer some 2800 km of beach breaks, point breaks and reefs. Swells are generated by Antarctic lows in the South Atlantic. Depending on where you are heading, the water temperatures in South Africa can range from rather chilly (ice-cream-headaches!) around Cape Town and the West coast to nice and pleasant around Durban. The Cape of Good Hope splits the powerful swells hitting the coast in half and sends them up the West coast (Atlantic) and the East coast (Indian Ocean). For this reason the East coast mainly offers righthanders such as Victoria Bay and Jeffrey's Bay and the West coast mainly delivers lefts such as Elands Bay. There is good surf all year round, however, the best time for a trip to South Africa is in their autumn and winter from April to October. Winter offers constant swells and good conditions. The downside of winter is obviously the weather, which can be quite cool. Spring and summer (November to March) offer warmer temperatures, however, with less consistency on the surf side of things. Very strong North east winds on the East coast and strong South east winds (known as the Cape Doctor) around the Cape and on the West coast create many windswells during summer. They lack the power of the strong winter groundswells but can still be fun to surf. This said, with a little bit of luck you might even score a tropical storm swell on the East coast during summer.

The best way to get around in South Africa is no doubt by car. Fly into Cape Town or Durban and get yourself a hire car to start with. Wetsuit wise the Cape Town region requires at least a 3/2 steamer and if possible booties. In winter, hood and gloves (neoprene ones of course) are the go. Jeffrey's Bay also requires a steamer most times it breaks. Heading towards Durban the water gradually warms up and you need only a shorty or tube suit for the Durban summer. Booties are still worth taking to avoid cuts from rocks and reefs, but also protect you from sea urchins. Choosing your weapons (surfboards) should not be too hard. Summer requires a shortboard for surf up to 6 feet and winter definitely requires a big wave tool (a spot called Dungeons, near Hout Bay, offers some of the biggest and heaviest waves on the planet).

This said, it is not a bad idea to buy surf equipment locally. Prices are generally pretty competitive and depending on what the South African Rand is doing there are some real bargains to be made.

The countless surf spots in South Africa can be separated into seven general areas: West coast, Cape peninsula, Southern cape (Garden Route), Jeffrey's bay area, Eastern cape, Wild coast and KwaZulu-Natal. We are just going to pick a few highlights to give you an overview, but if you are really want to dive into all the details we recommend Steve Pike's "Surfing in South Africa". This guidebook has many good tips on travelling in South Africa in general, but more importantly very detailed descriptions of the numerous surf spots. A great book but unfortunately it does not contain any maps, so get one of them locally as well.

The region around Cape Town offers around 50 different surf spots within an hours drive. Besides the well known spots like Glen Beach, the Reef/Point breaks at Kommetjie (Inner and Outer Kom), Llandudno with its barreling sandbar pounders and of course the legendary big wave break Dungeons you will be able to find some uncrowded but excellent beach and point breaks in one of the many bays in this area. So going for a surf check is actually a good thing to do.

This is no different in the region around Durban, the home of surfing legend Shaun Thomson. Besides the big names near towns such as Bay of Plenty (this used to be one of the best waves in the country before they added some new piers), North Beach, Dairy Beach, New Pier and Wedge it is well worth exploring the coast. The water temperature is pleasant and the climate almost tropical. Unfortunately the area is also notorious for our friends in the grey suits, but shark nets at the main beaches provide some ease of mind.

We are not giving away any secrets by telling you that the number one wave in South Africa is Jeffrey's Bay (J-Bay). J-Bay lies about 100 kilometres south of Port Elizabeth on the East coast, and is one of the longest and most perfect waves in the world. It breaks onto a sandy covered rock shelf. J-Bay is just like a machine, and produces one perfect wave after the other. Two or three tubes on one wave are possible. J-Bay point has four almost separate waves that with the right swell direction and size can connect to one incredible long ride, that is if you make it past a section called Impossibles (the name speaks for itself). The different waves are called Boneyards, Supertubes (of which Impossibles is a section), Tubes and Point. The main wave, and what you would usually see in the magazines, is Supertubes. J-Bay breaks along a reef shelf and ends after the Point section. There are stories of days where surfers rode even past the Point to a spot further down the line called Albatross. Remember from the take-off at Boneyards to Albtaross is about 1.2 km! In a good south west swell J-bay is like

a wave machine pumping out perfect wave after perfect wave. This place works anywhere between 4 and 12 feet. From 6-8 foot upwards the different sections start connecting and 2 to 3 tubes in one wave are nothing to get too excited about. It can be quite difficult to get out the back in bigger swells. There are only one or two keyholes in the reef shelf where the water is deep enough to paddle out. In particular at high tide they can be hard to locate

Llandudno South Africa

Pristine but freezing (Photo: Menges & Diel)

so it is wise to sit and watch for a while where everyone is paddling out or even ask one of usually friendly locals. Coming back in is a similar challenge with even experienced surfers sometimes ending up doing the rock dance.

The town of Jeffrey's Bay is actually not that small and you should find accommodation somewhere near the break. We can recommend "Supertubes Backpackers and Guesthouse" which sits right in front of the break.

Almost next door to J-Bay is Cape St. Francis. This break was made popular through the legendary movie the Endless Summer where Cape St. Francis was discovered as "THE" perfect wave. However people who surfed J-Bay wondered whether Bruce Browns movie team might have turned off the highway one exit to early. Perfect or not, Cape St. Francis is still always worth a soul searching trip.

We close this chapter with a few comments about sharks in South Africa. Not a pleasant topic, but one that can not be avoided when talking about surfing in this part of the world. Yep, they are all there, white pointers in the cold water around Cape Town and Tiger and Bullsharks in the warmer waters around Durban. There is no reason to go overboard on the countless shark stories, but a few safety precautions will not hurt either: Don't surf at dusk or dawn, don't surf near river mouths after extended rainfalls, don't surf with open wounds and do not urinate while out surfing (sharks are believed to sense distressed animals when they smell urine). One of the best things about South Africa, the many uncrowded spots, is at the same time one of the downsides. In particular if you are travelling by yourself it can be more then a little eerie to sit in a lonely line-up sharing the waves only with a few sharp teethed locals. But don't despair you are more likely to be struck by lightning playing a round of golf then you are being chewed on by a shark in South Africa.

Verskoon my, waar kann ek hier die perfekte golf find (afrikaans) = Excuse me, where do I find the perfect wave (Photo: Menges & Diel)

8 The Rest of the World

The rest of the world is obviously a huge area to cover and there is surf in the most incredible and sometimes remote areas. Everyone knows the hot spots like Hawaii, Australia or California. But who would have thought there is surf on the coast of the Easter Islands or in Alaska and that you can surf on the Amazon or in the Middle of Munich, Germany on the Ice-river? We couldn't possible mention every country or region that you can surf in so we thought we would pick a few cherries out of the big global surf cake.

Maldives

You are going on a surf trip to the Maldives? This was still the usual puzzled question you got a few years ago when you planned your surf trip to this chain of islands otherwise known for 5 Star holiday resorts with beautiful yet waveless beaches. However, once O'Neill put on a World Qualifying Series (WQS) surf contest in the Maldives, the word was out that there were some pretty

(Photo: "Dr. Surf" Thomas Herold)

There is a perfect wave waiting for everyone, somewhere

Maldives

hot (literally) waves to be found around some of the outer atolls. The best time is usually their wet season between May and October. The waves are generally in the 3-5 foot area and rarely get over 8 feet. Most waves break on rather forgiving reefs and offer perfect conditions for trying out the latest new school manoeuvre or simply improving your skills in almost machine like conditions. The climate ranges from warm to very warm and the same is true for the water temperature. The surf spots are all located on the outer islands of the atolls on the east side of the Maldives. The islands are positioned like pearls on a string across the equator from north to south. The most popular spots are in the North Male Atoll which also tends to get the most swell. The Atolls further south are usually referred to as "Outer Atolls", get less swell but also much lesser crowds as they can only be reached by boat charter.

As the Maldives mainly consist of either uninhabited or Hotel islands (except for the capital city Male which for a surfer is really a bit of a waste of time) booking your accommodation ahead is essential. To hop on a plane and sort everything out once you get there is simply not on. There are really only two alternatives: a Surf resort or a boat charter.

The best value for money in the Maldives is still (even after major renovations in 2006) Lohifushi Island. The resort is one of two Hotels with a private wave directly on your doorstep, accessible simply by paddling out. The break is called Lohis and is a fun left usually breaking around 4 feet on a mellow reef. It does get bigger occasionally when some perfect, deep blue tubes can be had. From Lohifushi there are also regular boat trips (in a so-called Dhoni) taking you to one of the 6 classy breaks nearby (Cokes, Chickens, Jails, Ninjas, Sultans or Honkeys – our favourite when its bigger and starts connecting with the tubey inside). There is usually a surf guide at the resort who is the key contact for organising the boat trips to these breaks. Otherwise Lohifushi is pretty much your average little paradise island with beautiful white beaches, great diving and snorkelling and of course plenty of honeymooners. As most goods in the Maldives are imported and then transported by boat to the various islands, it is little surprising that the Maldives are definitely on the expensive side of things (approximately US $ 10 for a simple rice dish). Best value for money usually offers all (or at least two meals) inclusive deals. Still then the cost of bottled water or a few drinks at sunset are sure to burn a good sized hole into your travel budget.

Other then Lohifushi there is really only the new Dhonveli Spa in terms of surf resorts. Dhonveli also has its private break called Pasta Point, which is definitely one of the better waves in the Maldives. However recent visitors have confirmed that apparently you need to buy something like a daily surf pass (even if you are staying on the island) which does not come cheap. So we strongly advise to double check with your booking agent that in fact the cost of surfing Pasta Point is included in the price you are paying. Dhonveli is definitely not for the budget minded surfer. If you are going to choose any other island in the North Male Atoll make sure they have a Dhoni on the islands that can take you to one of the nearby breaks. Paddling is definitely out of the questions (except for Lohis and Pasta) not only because of the distance but also because of the sometimes very strong currents between islands on incoming or outgoing tides (you will notice this while you are surfing anyway).

A different way of exploring the Maldives is via boat charter. 8-10 days are definitely enough to surf around the North Male Atolls, however a little more time is required for a trip that includes the Outer Atolls as considerable time is often spent travelling north or south. The most important thing though is to make sure that a surf guide is on the boat with you. There are a number of boats with non-surfing skippers who simply converted from taking divers out to the reef to taking surfers out to the waves. If you are unlucky enough, your skipper will simply take you to the most popular spots not even considering direction of wind and swell or what the tide is doing.

We have tried both options resort and charter. It is hard to say which one is better or worse. If the swell is small you are better off at the standard breaks for which you really do not need to stay on a boat. If you go in the main season, chances are that you are going to score a bigger swell and the Outer Atolls will come alive. A surf charter will then allow you to escape the crowds and surf some remote spots with just you and your friends on it.

To sum up, if you do have the extra cash that is required for surfing the Maldives it is definitely worth it – surf resort or boat charter. Incredibly fun waves and warm crystal clear water are what makes the Maldives another surf highlight in the Indian Ocean. Ahh and if perfect 4 foot waves do not bring your adrenalin level up, landing on a narrow runway, built onto a tiny island in the middle of the ocean, with a Jumbo Jet definitely will.

Réunion

The surf spots on Réunion are all concentrated on the west side of the island. There are about 10-12 spots, of which the majority are reef breaks. The swells come in from the south to southwest originating in the Antarctica with its violent storms. The best time to visit is between June and September. Outside of winter (June to August) where you may need a bit of rubber (shorty) the water is usually board short material. The best wave no doubt is St. Leu which breaks along a shallow coral reef directly into a beautiful calm bay. Booties are an absolute necessity as the reef is covered with sea urchins. St. Leu breaks from 3–8 foot and offers long intense rides. It can get rather crowded and hectic. Aaah, and there is the odd shark too. It is definitely a wave for the advanced surfer. Finding value for money accommodation is a bit of a problem on Réunion. The beach resorts are extremely pricey and really do not fit the average surfer's budget. Acceptable accommodation can be found in the hills about an hour away from the surf with some of the local families. In St. Leu itself, you either have to camp out under the trees on the beach (sounds better than it really is in this case), or rent an apartment.

Costa Rica

Costa Rica has waves all year round on two different coasts and oceans. The Pacific side, which is well developed and easy going and the somewhat more adventurous Caribbean side with heavy waves and some heavy vibes. The tropical climate, warm water and a great variety of waves make Costa Rica a true dream destination for surfers. The generally friendly locals (Ticos), inexpensive and good food as well as accommodation for every budget complete a positive picture.

The usual port of arrival is San José with Costa Rica's main airport. Do not waste too much time hanging around the big city but rather head of towards the ocean as soon as possible. We usually drive straight south to Jaco after an evening arrival (about 2 hrs from San Jose). This means we can hit the surf first thing in the morning. Another option is to head north to Tamarindo (about 5 hrs drive or catch a local plane as Tamarindo has a small airport). Whatever you do you will definitely need a hire car, preferably a four-wheel drive due to the sometimes nightmarish road conditions. Of course the hire companies know very well where the demand is, so do not expect any bargains on your Jeep. Costa Rica has two main seasons: Dry season from December to April and the Wet season from May to November. Both have their advantages and disadvantages. During the wet season the surf is much more consistent, accommodation is cheaper and the spots are less crowded. However, there is no way around paying extra for a 4-wheel drive hire car to be able to steer around and through some of the lake-sized mud puddles. Some spots actually become totally inaccessible by car and can only be reached by boat. This is the case with a place called Witches Rock north of Tamarindo which was made famous by the movie Endless Summer II (a trip is worth about 150 USD per boat carrying around 4 surfers).

The upside of the dry season is definitely the easy access to most breaks by car but also the frequent clean conditions with offshore winds however at the price of somewhat smaller swells, larger crowds and often more expensive or even fully booked accommodation. But don't worry. No matter what the season is when you land in San Jose, Costa Rica has everything you need.

The Pacific side has many quality point breaks and endless often empty beach breaks. However, the waves rarely get big (over 6 foot) or too radical. Dry season swells come from the south, wet season ones from the north. The most popular areas up north are on the Nicoya Peninsula around Mal Pais and Tamarindo. Both areas offer a great variety of waves. On the central Pacific coast Jaco and Quepos are the most reliable. Further south you will find Domenical, another surf haven with loads of quality beach breaks. Last but not least heading way south in the direction of Panama you will find Costa Rica's longest wave, Pavones.

The Caribbean side offers quite a different menu. There is a range of sometimes pretty heavy reef breaks that really start firing in the dry season. However the crime rate on this side of Coast Rica can be a problem so it's worth keeping your eyes open, in and out of the surf. This is really in contrast to the Pacific side that is really one of the safest and most relaxed places in Central America. General hygiene is adequate and you do not have to worry too much about whether you should have your drink with or without ice or what sort of water they use to wash the salad in restaurants. Scary tropical diseases are also not an issue. Another big bonus is the incredible wildlife. Costa Rica is one of the places where you actually get to see most of the exotic animals that you spotted in your travel guide book (make sure to check out the lazy crocodiles sunbathing on the banks of a river as you cross the river Tarcoles just north of Jaco). The constantly active Arenal Volcano is another cool place to check out. Also Costa Rica is one of the places where getting up for the dawn patrol is never an issue as the local coffee will even wake up the dead. Go there! Costa Rica is simply a lot of fun and pura vida.

Mexico

Mexico offers two alternatives for the surf hungry traveller. There is the Baja California and the mainland of Mexico. All spots are on the Pacific Coast, with the exception of Veracruz in the Gulf of Mexico. In the summer months the spots receive swell from the tropical cyclones which come up from the south. In winter the swell is generated by storms in the North Pacific off the coast of Mexico. By the way these are the same storms which pound the north shore of Hawaii in winter. There are surfers, who surf the swell in Hawaii, and then fly off to Mexico to ride on practically the same swell further south. In summer you should choose the southern tip of the Baja or the mainland of Mexico. In winter you surf the northern part of the Baja. The spots directly on the US American-Mexican border are usually packed with people on weekends. Mexico has every type of wave: from the absolute mind-blowing big wave spot on Todos Santos Island to the sand dredging tubes of Puerto Escondido, and the point breaks such as "Shipwrecks" near Cabo San Lucas. Cabo San Lucas is a popular party town with American surfers and marlin fishers. It sits on the southern tip of the Baja.

Finding somewhere to stay overnight is not difficult. There is also no lack of surf spots and nightclubs around the neighbourhood of Cabo. Do not miss the "Cabo Wabo" and the "Squid Roe". There is an absolutely awesome wave breaking in the north of the Baja on the island of Todos Santos, which lies just off Ensenada. Its name "Killers", hits the nail right on the head. You can only reach this break by boat. Here is where the big wave riders meet annually to charge the 20-foot plus monster waves. Last but not least there is the most famous wave on mainland Mexico at Puerto Escondido – the Mexican Pipeline. This little fishing village is about 50 minutes by plane or ten hours by bus from Mexico City. The waves break on a sandy bottom at Playa Zicatela. You will think, "Only a beach break!". You could not be more wrong, because the sand is so hard that the waves break like they do on a reef. This is one of the few beach breaks that holds waves up to 12 feet without things getting out of control. In a big swell and with your belly churning (not just from the burritos) you can surf smaller waves further inside the bay. Trust us, the closer you get to the harbour, the better your belly will feel. So, "Vamos amigos!"

TIP

9 Boat Trips

Over the last years a different kind of surf travel has evolved. These days surf magazines and movies are full of images taken on board chartered surf boats cruising trough exotic waters in Indonesia or elsewhere. These boats offer the luxury of air conditioning, TV, ice cold beer and maximum mobility in the middle of some of the most remote regions. Besides the obvious pleasures onboard a fully equipped yacht, the cool thing about boat trips is the absolute focus on surfing and the amount of time you will spend in the water. The boats anchor next to the surfspots and a small dinghy taxis back and forth between mothership and line-up all day. Eat-surf-drink-sleep, that's it. The boat crews take care of the rest including feeding the hungry surfer pack. Usually the water is warm and the waves are perfect. The evening chill-out session on deck with a cold

(Photo: "Dr. Surf" Thomas Herold)

hill out with tales
f chrystal swells

drink and all the stories of barrels, drop-ins and wipe-outs are classic. Because this way of surf travelling has really taken off, some of the most popular boat trip destinations like the Mentawais have become pretty busy. Imagine flying half way around the world, sitting in a shuttle bus for hours and sailing for another 12 hours before you arrive at a perfect wave with 10 other boats sitting in the same bay. Half of them probably loaded with professional surfers on a photo shoot. Not quite the picture you had in your mind when you booked your trip over the web. This said there are still plenty of areas and waves to be explored and, depending on the local knowledge of your skipper, he will be able to navigate around the crowds in many cases anyway.

At first only few professionals where invited to hop on board the by now legendary "Indies Trader" with skipper Martin Daley. Today everyone with web access can book him and his buddies on a boat charter in Northern Sumatra. Usually the boats can cater for around ten surfers plus a few non-surfing partners at a time. Where you want to go depends largely on the type of waves you are looking for, the time of the year you are planning to go and obviously the availability on board the boat of your choice. Bookings are done and paid for well in advanced, usually somewhere around 6 months ahead of departure. The prices obviously vary depending on the type of boat you charter. Somewhere in the order of US $ 150 per day including all meals is standard. Alcohol is usually extra and it is well worth checking the prices in advance as some boats e.g. in the Maledives are known to charge an arm and a leg. Another tip is to make sure to go for a boat with an experienced surfer-skipper. Because of the good money involved many boats have been transformed into surf charters and end up taking surfers simply to all the well-known breaks. If these are crowded or just not working these boats quickly run out of options. Also, make sure to carry a little more then a few band aids and mercurochrome with you. Medical help is often far away, and while many boat crews can handle and treat minor injuries, it is good to carry a good selection of standard medication against diarrhoea and maybe some antibiotics with you. Some places also require malaria medication despite the fact that you are actually staying on a boat with usually much lower malaria risk then on land. No doubt, boats will continue to push the final surf frontier over years to come. What are you waiting for, come aboard.

The world is covered with surf spots and actually any land with a coast has waves, whether it is in the Pacific, the Atlantic, the Indian Ocean or in the Mediterranean. Day in, day out, somewhere in the world, countless undiscovered and yet unsurfed waves are breaking. The surfer's eternal dream is to find the perfect yet secret spot – a perfect wave with no other surfers in sight. Somewhere out there this place still exists and is ready for you to discover it. You just have to get off your couch, pack your boards and go looking. But wherever you go don't forget to:

Surf hard and respect your environment!

(Photo: Bill Morris, O'Neill)

Surf hard and respect the ocean!

Occy, still ripping after all these years

(Photo: Kelly Smith. Smico, Surfer: Mark Occilupo)

V COMPETITIVE SURFING, SURF LINGO AND INFORMATION

Competitive Surfing

Professional surfers are the measure of all things in this sport. They travel around the world and compete against each other at the most famous surf spots in the world (unfortunately not always in the best conditions though). The top 44 pros compete in a series of roughly 14 competitions (the number changes each year) on the ASP World Tour (WCT). The up-and-coming surfers have to collect enough points in the World Qualifying Series (WQS) in order to qualify for the following year's WCT.

A competition is all about the most radical manoeuvres on the best waves. The official criteria are: "A surfer must perform radical, controlled manoeuvres in the critical section of a wave with Speed, Power and Flow to maximize scoring potential. Innovative / Progressive surfing as well as Variety of Repertoire (manoeuvres), will be taken into consideration when rewarding points for waves ridden. The surfer who executes these criteria with the maximum Degree of Difficulty and Commitment on the waves shall be rewarded with the higher scores." Simple, eh? On the WCT two pros surf against each other in exactly timed heats. An independent group of judges gives a point score for each ride. Controlled tube rides usually score the highest. A manoeuvre where the surfer falls off, no matter how radical the manoeuvre might have been, does not count. Usually only the two best rides are added up and taken into account. The internet has really revolutionised the way we can watch the top surfers compete. In the old days you were either lucky to have a contest come near by where you usually surf or you would have to wait until magazines reported about it or videos showed some footage of professional contests. These days you simply have to go to www.aspworldtour.com and you can watch all the WCT contests live over the internet. You can see the scores, get expert commentary usually from former pros and on top send real time text messages to the commentators. The fact that you are able to not only see all the surfing, but also see the live scores versus time remaining in a particular heat often provides great suspense and entertainment. Despite the fact that an event may be held in an exotic and remote location with hardly any spectators on site, millions will be following the event live over the web.

There are a number of surfers out there who can match it with the best in the world, but who are, however, not very successful in competitions. On the one hand this is often because they find it hard to surf under competition pressure and on the other to fulfil the criteria the judges are looking for. If the surfer falls off during a manoeuvre, irrespective of how radical it was, he does not receive any points for it. A tube ride only counts when the surfer emerges from the tube irrespective of how long he had been in the tube before. This means that professional surfers have to develop a radical, but nevertheless controlled surfing style for competitions.

Being able to handle the pressure to deliver high scoring rides while the time is ticking away is another key aspect required to become a surfing champion. Also the often festival-like party atmosphere surrounding the events has been the stumbling block for many young hot rookies over the years. Staying committed and professional is what often distinguishes a great surfer from a true champion.

However pro-surfing has produced a number of great champions over the years. Here are only a few that we think you must know:

Kelly Slater (USA)

The eight times World Champion – who can only be beaten by Flipper. Had a role in Baywatch and is the pop star of the surfing tour. He can do everything – big waves, tubes, small wave tricks etc.

Andy Irons (Haw)

Born on Kauai (Hawaii) Andy grew up with radical reef breaks and big waves. Competing with his younger brother Bruce - also a top surfer on the WCT - helped him to become a terrifying competitor. He has an amazing combination of big wave skills and small wave ripping and with his 3 world titles he is much more then just the "next Slater".

Tom Curren (USA)

In the 1980s he was three times World Champion. He is a master of the smooth style and competition strategy. He has the ultimate touch. Once, someone described him by saying "Tom Curren is the ocean".

Tom Carroll (Aus)

Two time World Champion. No one surfs powerful waves like he does. He matches power with power. His surfing at "Pipeline" belongs to the best ever.

Mark Occilupo (Aus)

The freak. He always had the misfortune in the 1980s to have to compete against Tom Curren, and therefore missed out on the World Championship. Curren has now retired, but 'Occy' came back and battled it out with the new schoolers to become the 1999 world champion. Well done mate!

Layne Beachley (Aus)

The dominant female surfer on the ASP Women's World Tour and with 7 World Champion titles one of the best female surfers of all time. The Australian born Beachley is the most powerful and most committed female competitor of her generation. A few tips from ex boyfriend Ken Bradshaw, the big wave and tow-in legend from Hawaii, might have helped her to become Kelly Slater's equivalent on the Women's World Tour.

"Sl8ter" - eight times World Champion

Kelly Slater

(Photo: Jeff Hornbaker, Quiksilver)

World Champions

Year	Men	Year	Women
1976	Peter Townend (Aus)	1976	N/A
1977	Shaun Tomson (Safr)	1977	Margo Oberg (Haw)
1978	Wayne Bartholomew (Aus)	1978	Lynne Boyer (Haw)
1979	Mark Richards (Aus)	1979	Lynne Boyer (Haw)
1980	Mark Richards (Aus)	1980	Margo Oberg (Haw)
1981	Mark Richards (Aus)	1981	Margo Oberg (Haw)
1982	Mark Richards (Aus)	1982	Debbie Beacham (USA)
1983	Tom Carroll (Aus)	1983	Kim Mearig (USA)
1984	Tom Carroll (Aus)	1984	Freida Zamba (USA)
1985	Tom Curren (USA)	1985	Freida Zamba (USA)
1986	Tom Curren (USA)	1986	Freida Zamba (USA)
1987	Damien Hardman (Aus)	1987	Wendy Botha (Safr)
1988	Barton Lynch (Aus)	1988	Freida Zamba (USA)
1989	Martin Potter (GB)	1989	Wendy Botha (Aus)
1990	Tom Curren (USA)	1990	Pam Burridge (Aus)
1991	Damien Hardman (Aus)	1991	Wendy Botha (Aus)
1992	Kelly Slater (USA)	1992	Wendy Botha (Aus)
1993	Derek Ho (Haw)	1993	Pauline Menczer (Aus)
1994	Kelly Slater (USA)	1994	Lisa Andersen (USA)
1995	Kelly Slater (USA)	1995	Lisa Andersen (USA)
1996	Kelly Slater (USA)	1996	Lisa Andersen (USA)
1997	Kelly Slater (USA)	1997	Lisa Andersen (USA)
1998	Kelly Slater (USA)	1998	Layne Beachley (Aus)
1999	Mark Occilupo (Aus)	1999	Layne Beachley (Aus)
2000	Sunny Garcia (Haw)	2000	Layne Beachley (Aus)
2001	C. J. Hobgood (USA)	2001	Layne Beachley (Aus)
2002	Andy Irons (Haw)	2002	Layne Beachley (Aus)
2003	Andy Irons (Haw)	2003	Layne Beachley (Aus)
2004	Andy Irons (Haw)	2004	Sofia Mulanovich (Peru)
2005	Kelly Slater (USA)	2005	Chelsea Georgeson (Aus)
2006	Kelly Slater (USA)	2006	Layne Beachley (Aus)

Surf Lingo

360: A 360 (three-sixty) degree turn on the wave

A-Frame: A wave that breaks perfectly left and right from the peak in the shape of a capital letter A.

Aerial: A manoeuvre where the surfer launches off the lip of the wave, is airborne for a short moment, and lands back on the wave

Aerial with Re-entry: After launching into the air the surfer turns his board in the air so that he is able to drop back into the wave and continues down the line.

Air to Fakie: Landing with the tail of the board pointing forward after an aerial. This often causes the surfer to briefly surf backwards after landing before spinning 180 to continue his ride.

Air: After a good bottom turn with a lot of speed, the rider cuts up the face, off-the-lip, and into the air

Aloha: Hawaiian word for hello or goodbye. Also Aloha spirit as in peaceful, friendly attitude towards life

Artificial Reef: A submerged human made object that causes waves to break where they otherwise would not.

Ate it: A wipe-out

Atoll: A coral island consisting of a belt of coral reef, partly submerged, surrounding a central lagoon.

Average Wave Period (AWP): The average distance (measured in seconds) between waves in a swell observed during a given period.

Backside: (to surf on the backhand) Surfing with one's back to the wave face

Barrel: See Tube

Barrel Roll: Type of aerial, but a 360-degree roll is added while in the air above the lip.

Backdoor: To pull into the tube from behind the peak. Also the righthander wave at the famous spot Pipeline (Hawaii).

Backside Air: An aerial performed on the surfer's backside.

Backwash: A wave is pushed back out to sea after breaking on the beach or rebounded off a pier or jetty.

Bail: To let go of the surfboard to avoid a wipe-out or being hit by a broken or breaking wave.

Balsa: Very light wood used in the '50s as a standard material for surfboards. Later replaced by polyurethane foam.

Beach break: Waves breaking on sand

Big waves: Large waves over 10 feet

Blank: Foam block used as the base material to shape a surfboard.

Blown Out: Condition where the wind is blowing so hard that it chops up the surf rendering the waves unsurfable

Board bag: A protective travel bag for the surfboard

Bodyboarder: Also called a Boogie boarder. A surfer who rides a short soft foam board lying down or kneeling

Bomb: An unusual big or close out wave.

Boomer: A wave larger than the average size on a particular day in a group of waves (also boomer-set)

Bottom-turn: A turn at the bottom of the wave face

Break: Area in the water where a wave breaks. Also a general expression for surfing beach (surf spot)

Bumpy: Choppy water on the face of the wave making it difficult to catch or ride the wave.

Buoy: A measuring device floating on the ocean surface. It can measure wind speed and direction, swell direction, period, duration, pressure and temperature.

Carving: Surfing through a turn on the rails of the surfboard, (also as a compliment; this guy is carving).

Catch a rail: To lose balance during a manoeuvre caused by incidentally digging the rail into the wave

Caught inside: An incoming set breaks in front of the surfer who has to dive or duck-dive through it

Channel: Area where no waves are breaking due to deep water or a current. Also grooves on the underside of the board designed to increase speed.

Charger: A radical surfer.

Chops: Uneven, whipped up surface on the water

Cleanup Set: A set of waves that break further out form the line-up and "cleans up" all surfers waiting for waves in the line-up.

Close-out: A wave that breaks along its whole length simultaneously – not ideal for surfing

Consistent: Condition where waves break in a regular interval. Also regions or surf spots can be consistent meaning they often receive good waves.

Crest: The top part of a wave.

Crowd: Large number of surfers in the water

Curl: The top part of the wave (lip) that curled already

Current: A flow of water along a beach, a pier or a reef (parallel or out flowing).

Custom-made: A surfboard designed and shaped particularly for the individual

Cutback: A turn that takes the surfer back from the shoulder into the pocket of the wave

Dawn patrol: Early morning surf session

Ding: A cut, crack or bump on the surface of the surfboard

Double Overhead: Wave measurement. A wave that is roughly two times taller than the surfer.

Drop-in: Stealing the right of way of another surfer. Also the take-off in a half-pipe on a skateboard

Drop: riding down the wave immediately after the take-off

Duck-dive: Advanced technique to get through a wave with the surfboard

Epic: Great surf session or conditions.

Epoxy: A plastic resin used by shapers as an alternative to polyester resin.

FCS: Fin Control System. Removable fins screwed into the board as opposed to being laminated in.

Fade: To surf in the opposite direction of the breaking wave direction after the take-off. Usually done to stall for a tube.

Fibreglass: Thin woven glass thread used in surfboard lamination.

Fins: Devices on the bottom of the surfboard to keep control while surfing.

Fish: Surfboard with a specially shaped swallowtail. Tom Curren has made this popular again

Flat: No waves (almost lake type conditions).

Floater: A manoeuvre allowing the surfer to glide over the white water of a breaking wave

Foam: The white water of a breaking wave. Also the material used as a surfboards' core.

Frontside: (to surf on the forehand) Surfing facing the wave

Full deck: Grip deck for both the rear and the front foot

Full suit: Also called a 'Steamer'. A wetsuit with long arms and long legs

Glassy: Smooth water surface resulting from absolutely calm wind conditions

Gnarly: Surf slang for a heavy or intimidating wave or situation.

Goofy: Also called 'goofy-foot'. A surfer who surfs with the right foot forward

Green room: See 'Tube'

Grip deck: Rough material fixed on the upper side of the surfboard, as a substitute for wax, to stop one slipping off the board

Grommet: Also called 'Gremmie'. A very young surfer

Groundswell: Strong swell caused by a violent storm far away off the coast

Gun: A big wave board

Hang Loose: Used to be a greeting amongst surfers in particular in Hawaii with a "Shaka" handshake. Also a relaxed state of mind.

Hang Ten: Manoeuvre usually used by longboarders where the surfer stands tall right on the tip of the board and all ten toes are placed on the nose.

Hardcore surfer: A dedicated radical surfer

Head High: Wave measurement. A wave that is roughly as tall as a surfer during a bottom turn.

Hit the Lip: The moment when a surfer does a turn on the falling portion of the wave (lip) before continuing down the line.

Hold Down: The time a surfer is held down underwater by a wave after a wipe-out.

Hollow wave: Wave with a steep and concave face

Hybrid: A mixture of long and shortboard

Impact zone: The point where the lip of the wave meets the surface of the water

Inside rail: The side of the surfboard nearest to the wave face. During a tube ride only the inside rail holds the board in the wave

Inside: The end of a wave where it meets reefs or points. Sitting on the inside – sitting close to the breaking edge of the wave. The surfer on the inside has priority

Isobars: Lines on a weather chart describing areas with equal atmospheric pressure.

Jetty: A structure usually consisting of rocks dividing a beach in separate parts or bordering both sides of an inlet or river-mouth.

Kick Out: To exit a wave with the board still under the surfers feet.

King tide: Extreme differences in the tide that occurs only on a few days in the year

Kneeboard: A board especially designed for riding in a knee stance.

Kook: Beginner or inexperienced surfer.

Laminate: Resin that is applied to a shaped surfboard blank and is soaked up the fibreglass mats.

Late take-off: A difficult start of a ride where one waits until the wave is extremely steep before standing up

Layback: Laying back into the face of the wave while surfing on the backside. Layback tubes used to be one of the coolest manoeuvres in the water.

Leash: A cord fixed to the ankle that attaches the board to the surfer

Line-up: The point in the water where the waves break and surfers wait for the wave. Also an orientation point on land as seen from the water

Lip: The front edge of the breaking wave where all the power is concentrated

Localism: Unfriendly behaviour by the locals towards surfers from outside

Locals: The local surfing community. Surfers who regularly surf at a particular spot.

Longboarder: Surfer who uses a long Malibu board in the classical style

Malibu: Name of a longboard and a famous point break in California

Mini-Malibu: Name of a mid-sized surfboard with the characteristic similar to a longboard.

Mushy waves: Waves whipped up by the wind

New school: A new radical way of surfing: aerials, tail-slides, reverse-surfing etc.

Neoprene: Material a wetsuit is made of.

North shore: The Mecca for surfers on the north coast of Oahu/Hawaii with many famous surf spots such as Pipeline, Sunset Beach and Waimea Bay

Nose-dive: The tip of the board digs into the water; usually ends up in a wipe-out

Nose: The front of the board

Offshore: When the wind is blowing from the land onto the sea creating a smooth surface on the wave face

Off-the-lip: A manoeuvre whereby a top-turn is made directly onto the lip of a breaking wave

Old School: Used to describe a traditional style of surfing e.g without aerials and tailslides

Ollie-hop: An expression borrowed from skateboarders to express a small aerial jump

Onshore: When the wind is blowing from the sea onto the land and creating choppy conditions

Outside: Reference is the line-up. Outside means further out to sea respectively beyond the area where the waves usually break.

Overhead: When the wave is higher than the surfer standing on his board

Over the falls: Situation of getting sucked into the lip after a late duck dive or a wipe-out and fall over with it as the wave breaks.

Peak: Top of a wave; the highest point of a wave. Similarly also a wave breaking to the right and the left (A - frame peak)

Peeling: A wave breaks perfectly from the start all the way down the line like the skin of a fruit being peeled off in one piece.

Period: The time interval between waves.

Pigdog: Technique enabling a tube to be ridden on the backhand

Pintail: A tapered end of the surfboard

Pipeline: A surfspot on the North Shore in Hawaii with gnarly tubes breaking in shallow water

Pitch: The moment when the lip throws out to form a tube

Plug: An inlay at the tail of the board where the leash is attached

Point break: Where the wave breaks along a headland

Polyester: A most common type of plastic resin used in surfboard manufacturing.

Pro surfer: A professional surfer – abbreviated to 'pro'

Pumping: Build up speed by 'pumping' the board up and down on a wave

Quad: A surfboard with four fins

Rail: The edge of the surfboard

Rail, boxy: Thick or heavy rail. Designed for smaller waves and mostly used on hybrid boards or short boards shaped for heavy riders.

Rail, full: Standard shortboard rail.

Rail, thin: Thin or sharp rail. Designed for larger and/or hollow waves.

Rail grab: Holding onto the rail of a surfboard to keep control during a manoeuvre. Usually used during backside tube riding and aerials.

Rail saver: A piece of nylon at the end of the leash to protect the board from damage, or to prevent the fingers being squashed when pulling the board behind while diving through a wave

Rash: A skin irritation caused by the sun or rubbing

Rashguard: A polyester shirt used either to prevent a rash from the wetsuit or as a protection against the sun.

Re-entry: Also called 'Reo'. "See Off-the-lip"

Rebound: Also called 'Ricochet'. A turn executed on the breaking lip of the wave after a cutback in order to turn back into the 'right' direction

Reef break: Waves that break over reefs

Regular: Also called 'Regular foot'. A surfer who surfs with the left foot forward

Resin: A liquid plastic that hardens when mixed with a catalyst. Used in surfboard manufacturing to seal the shaped blank and to repair major dings or creases.

Rhino chaser: A large surfboard for big waves

Rip Tide: A strong out-flowing current.

Rip: Turbulent water but also see ripper.

Ripper: A radical exceptional surfer ("this guy rips").

Rocker: The curvature along the surfboard from the nose to the tail.

Rookie: A young hot up-and-coming surfer

Roundhouse Cutback: A cutback straight towards the breaking part of the wave followed by a rebound from the tumbling foam to turn back in the opposite direction again. All together the surfer will have surfed a full figure 8.

Secret spot: A 'secret' surfing beach with no surfers in the water

Section: A segment of the wave. To section: Several parts of the wave break down at once. Making it impossible to ride from start to end

Set: A group of waves

Sex Wax: One of the most popular surf wax.

Shape: The surfboard form

Shaper: Person who builds surfboards

Shore break: A wave that breaks directly onto the dry sand

Shortboard: A short surfboard about 6 feet long for performance surfing

Shoulder Hopper: To drop in on the shoulder of the wave to avoid a more difficult take-off on the main peak or section.

Sideshore: The wind is blowing parallel to the coastline.

Significant Wave Height: The average height of the highest 1/3 of the waves in a set.

Slash: A radical cutback or top turn performed on the face of the wave.

Slop: Bad, chopped-up waves

Skimboard: A small board without fins for sliding over the shallow film of water on the waters' edge.

Snaking: Competing unfairly or stealing the priority for a wave

Snap: A manoeuvre where the surfer executes a rapid violent turn at the top of the wave wall

Spinout: Situation when the fins lose contact to the water resulting in a loss of control

Spit: The spraying of mist out of the tube generated by the collapsing wave.

Spray: Water thrown or splashed up by a quick turn

Spring suit: A wetsuit with short arms and legs

Squash tail: A slightly squared tail with rounded corners.

Square tail: Straight rear end to the surf board. Standard form of the tail.

Stall: A braking or slowing ('stalling') movement in order to allow the tube to catch up

Standing wave: Usually found in rivers, where fast moving water rebounds off an immovable object underwater (i.e. stone).

Stick: A surfboard.

Stringer: A thin strip of wood let into the length of the board to add stability

Sucked Dry: A dangerous wave that sucks up the shallow water over a reef leaving the area in front of the wave nearly dry.

Sucky waves: Very steep waves that suck up the water from the base of the wave

Surfari: A 'wave hunting' trip. Originated from the African word safari

Surf camp: Accommodation that particularly caters for surfers at a good surfing spot

Surf check: Checking the waves from a spot on the beach

Surf session: The time spent in the water surfing

Surf spot: A beach suitable for surfing

Surfers (Swimmers) Ear: An effect that can appear after of long-term exposure to cold water and wind. It leads to an enlargement of the bone in the inner ear canal.

Swallow tail: The rear end of a surfboard shaped in the form of a swallow tail

Swell: Waves before they break

Swell Direction: The direction i.e. south, north etc. the swell is approaching from.

Switchfoot: A surfer who can surf regular or goofy foot just depending on the direction of the wave.

Tail slide: Placing pressure on the tail of the board during an extreme turn so that the rear end 'breaks' away

Tail: Rear end of the surfboard

Tanker: A thick and heavy surfboard.

Take-off: The start of a ride

Tidal Bore: Fast moving wave caused by an extreme tide influence between the ocean and the flowing water from rivers or estuaries. The most popular is the Pororoca in the Amazon.

Thruster: A surfboard with three fins positioned at the rear end of the board. One in the middle and one on each side

To backdoor: Taking (or entering) a tube from behind at high speed. The opposite is to 'stall' to get in the tube

To rip: Extreme radical way to surf. 'Ripper' – a very good surfer

Top-to-bottom wave: A wave that breaks directly from the top into the bottom of the wave. Generally this creates a tube

Top-turn: A turn executed on the top edge of a wave

Tow Board: A smaller but heavier surfboard designed specially for tow-in surfing. Usually enhanced with foot straps or bindings.

Tow-in: Being towed into a wave that is too large to paddle into by a Jetski.

Tube: A tunnel is formed behind the lip of the breaking wave and the rest of the wave. A surfer is able to surf for a short time in this space. The most popular manoeuvre for surfers

Tube suit: A wetsuit with short legs and a sleeveless vest shaped upper part

Volume: The buoyancy of the surfboard.

Wall: The face of a wave that has not yet broken

Wavelength: The Distance measured between successive wave crests.

Wax: Used on a surfboard deck to prevent slipping.

Wetshirt: Also called 'Rashguard'. A thin shirt made of Lycra to provide protection from the sun or rashes caused by rubbing the skin

Wetsuit: A surf suit made from Neoprene

White water: The foam of a broken wave

Width: The dimension of a surfboard from rail to rail.

Windswell: Weak swell created by winds near the coast (opposite is groundswell)

Wipe-out: To fall off the board

You Should Have Been Here Yesterday: A classical phrase to describe previous conditions of the day before to someone who missed it. Usually exaggerated by the surfer who has been there.

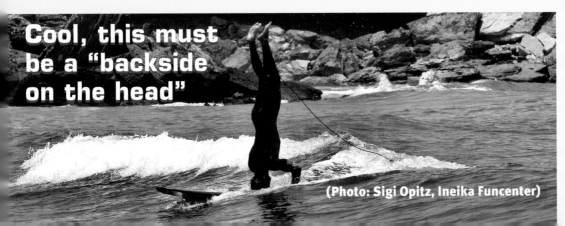

Cool, this must be a "backside on the head"

(Photo: Sigi Opitz, Ineika Funcenter)

Information

Surfrider Foundation USA
PO BOX 6010
San Clemente, CA 92674-6010 USA
Phone: +1 (949) 4 92-81 70
E-Mail: membership@surfrider.org
www.surfrider.org/

Surfrider Foundation Europe
20 av de Verdun
64200 Biarritz
France
Phone: +33 (0)5 59 23 54 99
Fax: +33 (0)5 59 41 11 04
www.surfrider-europe.org

This is an environmental organisation whose aim is to protect and look after the world's seas, waves and beaches. As a European surfer you can also support them through their European branch.

Surfaid International
www.surfaidinternational.org

The mission of SurfAid International, a non-profit humanitarian aid organization, is to improve the health of people living in isolated regions connected to us through surfing.

International

ASP - Association of Surfing Professionals www.aspworldtour.com
ISA - International Surfing Association www.isasurf.org

Europa

ASP Europe - Association of Surfing Professionals Europe
www.aspeurope.com
European Surfing Federation
www.eurosurfing.org

Germany

WAVETOURS
Uli Scherb and Martin Storck
Ludwigshöhstraße 37
64285 Darmstadt
Phone: + 49 (0)6151- 4 57 27
Fax: + 49 (0)6151- 42 50 52
E-Mail: info@wavetours.com
www.wavetours.com

Spain

Ineika Funcenter Fuerteventura
Surf school and camp by Sigi Opitz
35660 Corralejo,
Fuerteventura
Phone: +34 928 53 57 44
E-Mail: funcenter@ineika.de
www.ineika.de

Switzerland

Swiss Surfing Association
E-Mail: info@waveriding.ch
www.waveriding.ch

Sudden Rush
Chris Bachmann and Jürg Eggenberger
Forchstraße 226
8032 Zürich
Phone: +41-1-420 14 44
Fax: +41-1-420 14 41
E-Mail: info@suddenrush.com
www.suddenrush.com

Austria

Austrian Surfing Federation
E-Mail: Office@austriansurfing.com
www.austriansurfing.com

Portugal

The Surf Experience
Dago Lipke
P.O. Box 612
8600 Lagos
Phone: +351 2 82 76 09 64
Fax: +351 2 82 76 72 88
E-Mail: thesurfexperience@clix.pt
www.thesurfexperience.de

Australia

STC The Surf Travel Company
PO Box 446
Cronulla, NSW 2230
Phone: +61 2 95 27 47 22
Fax: +61 2 95 27 45 22
www.surftravel.com.au

Worl Surfaris
E-Mail: info@worldsurfairs.com
www.worldsurfaris.com

USA

WATERWAYS SURF ADVENTURES
E-Mail:
waterways@waterwaystravel.com
www.waterwaystravel.com

Wavehunters
2424 Vista Way
Oceanside, CA 92054
Phone: + 1 76 04 33 30 78
E-Mail:
wavehunters@wavehunters.com
www.wavehunters.com

Electra Bicycle Company
2262 Rutherford Road, Suite 104
Carlsbad, CA 92008, USA
Phone: +1 (760) 6 07-24 53
Fax: +1 (760) 6 07-24 56
www.electrabike.com

Indonesia

G-land
Jungle Surf Camp
E-Mail: g-land@sby.centrin.net.id
www.G-land.com

Bobbys Surfcamp
www.grajagan.com
Phone: +62 3 61 75 55 88
Fax: +62 3 61 75 56 90

Fiji

Tavarua Island Resort
Book through Island Tours
P.O. Box 60159
Santa Barbara, CA 93 160
USA
Phone: +1 8 05 6 86 45 51
Fax: +1 8 05 6 83 66 96

Namotu Island
(Blue Water Sports Resort)
WATERWAYS SURF ADVENTURES
E-Mail:
waterways@waterwaystravel.com
www.waterwaystravel.com
or directly: Namotu Island
P.O BOX 531 NADI, FIJI
Phone: (Fiji) 6 79-67 06-4 39
Fax: (Fiji) 6 79-67 06-0 39
E-Mail: namotu@connect.com.fj
www.namotuisland.net

Organisations:

www.surfaidinternational.com
www.aspworldtour.com
www.surfrider.org
www.surfrider-europe.org

www.isasurf.org
www.eurosurfing.org
www.aspeurope.com
www.surf-dwv.de/index.htm

Mags/Books/News:

www.surfermag.com
www.surfingthemag.com
www.surfersjournal.com
www.surfeuropemag.com
www.towsurfer.com
www.transworldsurf.com
www.tracksmag.com
www.surfinglife.net
www.surfersmag.de
www.epicsurf.de

www.meyer-meyer-sports.com
www.surfsession.com
www.orcasurf.co.uk
www.zigzag.co.za
www.surfingnz.com
www.lowpressure.co.uk
www.surfbooks.com
www.surferspath.com
www.surfersvillage.com/

Surf reports:

www.planetsurf.net
www.surftrip.net
www.surfhistory.com/
www.coldswell.com
www.the-daily-dose.com
www.wannasurf.com
www.surfline.com
www.realsurf.com
www.swell-line.com
www.coastalwatch.com.au

www.surf-report.com
www.stormsurf.com
www.wavewatch.co.za
www.baliwaves.com
www.surfrider.org/earth.htm
www.surf.co.nz
www.wavewatch.com
www.aquabumps.com
www.surfspot.co.uk/

Surf gear:

www.billabong.com
www.quiksilver.com
www.oneill.com
www.oneilleurope.com

www.surfgotcha.com
www.ripcurl.com
www.localmotionhawaii.com
www.tcsurf.com

www.rusty.com
www.smithoptics.com
www.oakley.com
www.arnette.com
www.dragonalliance.com
www.nixonnow.com
www.op.com
www.spyoptic.com
www.ezekielusa.com
www.alpinestars.com
www.oceanearth.com.au
www.jetpilot.com.au
www.lizzard.co.za
www.mambo.com.au
www.nofear.com
www.reef.com
www.stussy.com
www.toesonthenose.com
www.chiemsee.com
www.hurley.com
www.earthproducts.com
www.volcom.com
www.lostenterprises.com
www.freestyleusa.com
www.globe.tv
www.dcshoes.com
www.vans.com

www.vanssurf.com
www.etnies.com
www.etniessurf.com
www.sanuk.com
www.cobianusa.com
www.gravisfootwear.com
www.dvssurf.com
www.vonzipper.com
www.zooyork.com
www.havaianasus.com
www.fox-surf.com
www.splitusa.com
www.animal.co.uk
www.cultindustries.com
www.oxbowworld.com
www.flojos.com
www.rvcaclothing.com
www.adiosurf.com
www.analogclothing.com
www.mcd-surf.com
www.hottunaint.com
www.kustomfootwear.com
www.anonoptics.com
www.mauiandsons.com
www.honoluasurf.com
www.osirisshoes.com
www.electricvisual.com

Girls:

www.billabonggirls.com
www.roxy.com
www.volcom/girls.com

www.nikitaclothing.com
www.bodyglovegirls.com

Boards:

www.cisurfboards.com
www.brewersurf.com

www.byrnesurf.com
www.hicsurfshop.com

www.bicsport.com
www.hobie.com
www.alohasurfboards.au
www.alohasurfusa.com
www.surftech.com
www.buster-surfboards.com
www.pukassurf.com
www.semente.pt
www.waveridingvehicles.com
www.tcsurf-france.com
www.starksurf.com
www.lostenterprises.com
www.xanadusurfdesigns.com

www.surfindustries.com/webber
www.hiceurope.com
www.addictionsurfboards.com
www.classicmalibu.com
www.fatomsurfboards.com
www.shaping-room.com
www.insight51.com
www.jpsurfboards.co.uk
www.lindensurfboards.com
www.akasurf.com
www.surfprescriptions.com
www.naturalart.com
www.rustysurfboards.com

Training:

www.indoboard.com

www.vasatrainer.com

Wax/Fins/Wetsuits/Accessories:

www.xcelwetsuits.com
www.sexwax.com
www.dakine.com
www.surffcs.com
www.futuresfins.com
www.surfcohawaii.com
www.xtrak.com
www.bodyglove.com
www.creatures.com.au
www.neilpryde.com
www.oamsurf.com
www.gul.com

www.realmeurope.com
www.gotcha-europe.com
www.westsurfing.co.uk
www.islandstyle.co.za
www.g-grip.com
www.stickybumps.com
www.solarez.com
www.billabongwetsuits.com
www.patagonia.com/wetsuits
www.bubblegumsurfwax.com
www.headhuntersurf.com
www.t-raxsurf.com

Skateboards

www.sector9.com
www.gravityboard.com
www.arborsports.com

www.scskate.com
www.powell-peralta.com/

Travel:

www.quiksilvertravel.com
www.surftravel.com.au
www.worldsurfaris.com
www.waterwaystravel.com
www.mentawaiislands.com
www.surfex.com
www.bajasurfadventures.com

www.discoversurfing.com
www.atolltravel.com
www.lonelyplanet.com
www.wavescape.co.za
www.ticotravel.com
www.wavehunters.com
www.tropicsurf.net

Camps:

www.ineika.de
www.wavetours.com
www.thesurfexperience.de
www.suddenrush.com
www.easydrop.com

www.wellenreiter.com
www.fijisurf.com
www.surfbetter.com
www.witchsrocksurfcamp.com
www.nomadsurfers.com

Weather:

www.fnmoc.navy.mil/public/
www.noaa.gov

www.swell-forecast.com
www.windguru.com

Online shops:

www.stokeshop.com
www.swell.com
www.jackssurfboards.com
www.ronjons.com

www.surfride.com
www.killerdana.com
www.hsssurf.com
www.k5.com

DVD/Photo:

www.woodshedfilms.com
www.poorspecimen.com
www.jackjohnsonmusic.com
www.aaronchang.com
www.tim-mckenna.com
www.themoonshineconspiracy.com

www.thesurflab.com
www.surfphotogallery.com
www.extremsportsvideos.com
www.photosgrannis.com/
www.aframephoto.com/store
www.studio411.com

SURFING

Thanks to all those without whose help this book would not have been possible
In alphabetical order:

Benno and Jeano from Electra, Reinhard Bellet, Billabong Europe, Rick Doyle
Conny Jarosch, The Biarritz boys, "Dr. Surf" Thomas Herold, Ecki Hillebrecht
Family Diel, Family Menges, Fanatic, Meyer & Meyer Publishing, Jan "Leo"
Leopold, Dago and Marlon Lipke, Joli Productions, Kelly "Smico" Smith, Kuta Lines
O'Neill, Pete Longhurst, Quiksilver, Ashton Robinson, Quirin Rohleder, Roe
Welters, Roland Hansky, Sigi Opitz, Stefan "Muli" Müller, The State of Victoria
Tony King from STC, Uli and Martin from Wave Tours, Windsurfing Chiemsee and
our beloved and understanding wives Heidi and Natalie and our kids Luis, Elena
Henrik, Mika and Sebastian.
-and anyone we have forgotten to mention

Photo & Illustration Credits:

Cover Photo: O'Neill, Bill Morris
Cover Design: Jens Vogelsang, Germany
Photos inside: See Captions